John Lanne Buchanan

**Travels in the Western Hebrides**

From 1782 to 1790

John Lanne Buchanan

**Travels in the Western Hebrides**
*From 1782 to 1790*

ISBN/EAN: 9783337319397

Printed in Europe, USA, Canada, Australia, Japan

Cover: Foto ©Andreas Hilbeck / pixelio.de

More available books at **www.hansebooks.com**

# TRAVELS

IN THE

## *WESTERN HEBRIDES.*

# TRAVELS

IN THE

## *WESTERN HEBRIDES:*

FROM 1782 TO 1790.

BY THE

REV. JOHN LANE BUCHANAN, A. M.

MISSIONARY MINISTER TO THE ISLES FROM THE CHURCH OF SCOTLAND.

*LONDON:*

PRINTED FOR G. G. J. AND J. ROBINSON, PATERNOSTER-ROW; AND J. DEBRETT, OPPOSITE TO BURLINGTON HOUSE, PICCADILLY.

1793.

PRICE 3s. 6d.

# ADVERTISEMENT.

IT may be proper to apprise the reader, or rather those whom I wish to become readers, that the subject of this little volume is not those Islands that lie near to the coast of Scotland, but the *Western* Æbudæ; a long chain of islands a whole degree farther advanced in the Atlantic Ocean: seldom visited, and their interior œconomy, the situation, circumstances, and character of the people never before described by any modern traveller, except, in a very summary manner, by Donald Monro, quoted and followed by *George Buchanan,* in his

History

History of Scotland. I have been advised to give it the title of Travels, because the remarks it contains are the result of many voyages and journies, performed for a long feries of years: although I have avoided the *tædium* of a long chain of dates, movements, and other circumftances of no confequence.

What I have written, I well know, will give offence to many petty tyrants: but I am actuated by motives of humanity, and of duty to the common Parent and Lord of all mankind. And I thank God, who has given me grace to fpeak the truth with boldnefs, notwithftanding the menaces of certain unprincipled oppreffors.

If any perfon fhall think proper publicly to controvert the truth of any of the facts I have afferted, I requeft that he may fubfcribe his name to what he may write: in which cafe I will fupport my affertion, by producing the evidence on which I made it: but if it fhall be made to appear, that I was in any inftance mifled, I will acknowlege my error.---To anonymous writing I fhall not pay the fmalleft regard or attention.

I once intended to add, as an Appendix to this little Work, a Refutation of Mr. Pinkerton's outrageous calumnies againft the Celts in general, and the ancient Scots and modern Highlanders in particular. This has been delayed for the prefent, on account of certain unavoidable circumftances, unneceffary to be mentioned. But, the Public may expect to fee it foon in another Publication.

# CONTENTS.

*Page*

*INTRODUCTION* . . . . . . . 1

### CHAP. I.

*A Description of the Western Hebrides* 11

### CHAP. II.

*The political State of the Western Hebrides---The principal Proprietors---Tacksmen--Subtenants---Predial Slaves, or Scallags* 26

### CHAP. III.

*Tacksmen---Subtenants---Scallags---- Predial Slaves* . . . . . . . . . . . . . . 47

CHAP.

## CHAP. IV.

*Of the Genius, Customs Manners, and Dress of the Western Hebrideans* ...... 79

## CHAP. V.

*Of St. Kilda* ............ 118

## CHAP. VI.

*Modes, Implements, and general State of Husbandry* ...., ......... 147

## CHAP. VII.

*Of Marriages, Baptism, and Burials; with the several singular Ceremonies and Usages* 163

## CHAP. VIII.

*Oppressive Customs----Tenants fostering their Master's Children without Board Wages---Begging of Cows, Sheep, and Goats, after Marriage---Begging of Wool---Begging of Cocks---Anecdotes* .......... 171

CHAP.

## CHAP. IX.

*Anecdotes of Prince William Henry—Of the Town of Stornaway, in Lewis----Contrast between the Dawnings of Liberty and Comfort opened in Lewis, and the present State of the adjacent Island of Harris---Former Manners and Mode of Life in the Hebrides compared with the present.---A Comparison of the Condition of the Hebrideans, and other Highland Scallags, with that of the Negroes in the West-Indies---Observations on the Attempts to introduce extensive Fisheries into the Islands and Highlands of Scotland.* 186

## CHAP. X.

*State of Religion in the Western Hebrides--- Presbyteries---Synods---Missionaries---Elders —Schoolmasters---Catechists* .... 219

# INTRODUCTION.

THE diſtance of that part of the Hebrides called the Long Iſland, comprehending Lewis, Harris, both the Uiſts, Barray, and other ſmall Iſles, and the dangers of a voyage among iſlands, advanced to the diſtance of 70 miles from the main land of Scotland in a tempeſtuous ocean, account for the general ignorance of the manners, customs, characters, and political ſituation of thoſe wild and diſtant regions: which have of late been brought under the public eye, chiefly by the misfortunes of the inhabitants. Though ſeveral travellers have viſited Skye, Mull, Iſla, Jura, and other iſlands of ſmaller extent, ſkirting the weſtern ſhores of the main land, we have never yet had any written accounts of the Long Iſland, or rather chain of Islands; or, at least, any accounts relating to the domestic and political situation of the inhabitants. This indeed, is at present most deplorable: the relief of emigration, offered to some, being denied to the far greater number by extreme poverty; and a petty tyranny, arising from immemorial usages established in times of feudal oppression, and their singular and remote situation, which secludes the miserable natives of the Western Hebrides from the benign influence of the British laws and government. A right avails nothing without a remedy. The poor Hebridean, as well as the Highland cottager in the more sequestered parts of North-Britain, would find it impossible to effect, if he had courage to attempt, emancipation and independence on the tacksmen, and petty lairds or landholders, who keep them in subjection. I say petty lairds and tacksmen, for with regard to the great proprietors of land and sea-coast in those parts, Lord Macdonald,

Mr.

Mr. Humberstone Mackenzie, Captain Macleod of Harris, Mr. Macdonald of Boisdale, and a few other gentlemen of large estates, they have given undoubted proofs of a disposition to protect the great body of the poor people against their immediate superiors and oppressors; by enouraging general industry, which cannot exist without liberty, or, in other words, without justice. But it too often, and indeed for the most part happens, that non-residence, and various avocations, on the part of the great landholders, afford opportunities to the tacksmen, among whom their estates are divided, by leasehold, in large lots, or rather districts, to conceal the real state of affairs from the distant chief, and to enter into such combinations, as at once, in fact, frustrate the good intentions of those chiefs, and defy the free genius of the British constitution. The land is parcelled out in small portions, by the tacksmen, among the immediate cultivators of the soil, who pay their rent in kind, and in perfonal fervices. Though the tackfmen, for the moft part, enjoy their leafes of whole diftricts on liberal terms, their exactions from the fubtenants, are in general moft fevere. They grant them their poffeffions only from year to year: and, left they fhould forget their dependent condition, they are every year, at a certain term, with the moft regular formality, warned to quit their tenements, and to go out of the bounds of the leafehold eftate. The fubtenant, by what prefents he can command, or by humble fupplications, endeavours to work on the mind of the tackfman, and, on any condition he pleafes to impofe, to retain a home for himfelf, his wife and children; for he has no other refource. And here I am to difclofe to the Englifh nation, as well, I hope, as the greater part of the Scotch, and to the whole world, a matter of fact, which cannot fail to excite a very general fympathy

and

and concern for a sober, harmless, and much injured people.

It is an invariable custom, and established by a kind of tacit compact among the tacksmen and inferior lairds, to refuse, with the most invincible obduracy, an asylum, on their ground, to any subtenant without the recommendation of his landlord: or, as he is very properly called in those parts, his MASTER.\* The wretched out-cast, therefore, has no alternative, but to sink down into the situation and rank of

an

---

\* So inveterate are the remains of feudal slavery in Scotland, that MASTER is for the most part the term used for landlord. Mr. Kemp, a minister, in a sermon preached before the Society for Propagating Christian Knowledge, at their anniversary meeting in the High Church of Edinburgh, June 5, 1788, on the subject of the character of the late Earl of Kinnoull, calls him, in relation to his tenants, their MASTER. It was impossible for the Scotch orator to divest himself of the idea, that even the good and generous Kinnoull was not the landlord but the MASTER of his tenants, in the very sentence in which he considers us " free-born Britons." See Kemp's Sermons and Facts, page 117.

an unfortunate and numerous claſs of men known under the name of Scallags.

The ſcallag, whether male or female, is a poor being, who, for mere ſubſiſtence, becomes a predial ſlave to another, whether a ſubtenant, a tackſman, or a laird. The ſcallag builds his own hut with ſods and boughs of trees; and if he is ſent from one part of the country to another, he moves off his ſticks, and, by means of theſe, forms a new hut in another place. He is however, in moſt places, encouraged by the poſſeſſion of the walls of a hut, which he covers in the beſt way he can with his old ſticks, ſtubble, and fern. Five days in the week he works for his maſter: the ſixth is allowed to himſelf, for the cultivation of ſome ſcrap of land, on the edge of ſome moſs or moor: on which he raiſes a little kail, or cole-worts, barley, and potatoes. Theſe articles, boiled up together in one maſh, and often without ſalt, are his only food;

food; except in those seasons and days when he can catch some fish, which he is also obliged not unfrequently to eat without bread or salt. The only bread he tastes is a cake made of the flour of barley. He is allowed coarse shoes, with tartan hose, and a coarse coat, with a blanket or two for clothing. It may occur to an English reader, that, as the scallag works only five days out of seven to his master, he has two to provide for himself. But it is to be recollected, that throughout the whole of Scotland and all its appendages, as well as in the opposite countries of Iceland to the north, and Norway and Denmark to the east, Sunday, or the Sabbath, as it is called in all those countries, is celebrated by a total cessation from all labour, and all amusements too, as well as by religious exercises.

Although the Western Hebrides lie beyond the route pursued by the most distinguished

guished travellers from the south, who have published accounts of their travels and voyages, (Mr. Pennant, Dr. Johnson, and Captain Newte) several gentlemen, have visited most of those remote Islands, with a view of acquiring such local knowledge as might enable them to employ the people in a fishing trade, or other industry: though none of them ever touched on the horrid island of Harris. But the want of time, and their not being able to converse with the common people, who know no other language than the Celtic, and who alone could, or would point out their grievances in their native colours, the benevolent purpose of those gentlemen was, in a great measure, frustrated. The tacksmen, with whom they conversed, and their own factors, had an interest in concealing some truths, the knowledge of which might have equally benefited the independent freeholders, and the great body of the labouring people.

The Writer of the following notes, whofe commiffion from the Society for Propagating Chriftian Knowledge, from 1782 to 1791, gave him an opportunity of becoming acquainted with the actual fituation of affairs in the Weftern Hebrides, trufts, that he will do no differvice, but on the contrary promote the interefts of both the chiefs and the natives at large, by difclofing fcenes induftrioufly concealed from the eye of the benevolent Landholder, as well as of the inquifitive ftranger: in the hope that humanity and found policy may devife fome means for alleviating the miferies, and converting, to both public and private advantage, the induftry of a fober, harmlefs, and ingenious, but ill-treated people. The picture, on the whole, will be a melancholy one, but here and there relieved by fome curious manners and cuftoms, and fome particulars in natural hiftory.---
The Author could never boaft of any elegance of ftyle in compofition: but this, fuch as it was, has not, he is very fenfible, been

improved

improved by wandering about for nine years, where he very feldom heard or converfed in any other tongue than the Celtic. He has fet down fome things, as he heard them in this language; not knowing how to give their full meaning in Englifh.

# TRAVELS

IN THE

# WESTERN HEBRIDES.

## CHAP. I.

*A Description of the Western Hebrides.*

THIS great ridge of iſlands runs in a parallel line with the main land of Scotland, from Barray-head, the ſouthernmoſt point of the Iſland diſtinguiſhed by that name, to Niſh, the northern point of Lewis, about 180 miles in extent; and, in breadth, from 5 miles to 20. The whole of this vaſt ridge of iſles, which is fully ſtocked with inhabitants, is divided into eight pariſhes: in which there are, beſides the pariſh churches, three ſtations for Clerical Miſſioners ſupported by the royal bounty.

The weſtern ſides of Barray and Uiſt are flat and ſandy: the eaſtern, mountainous, and full of moſſes and rugged rocks. The inland parts are interſperſed with freſh-water lakes, and theſe plentifully ſtocked with fiſh. There are ſeveral ſmall rivers, in the mouths of which there is plenty of ſalmon, falling for the moſt part into the weſtern ſeas.

The leſſer Iſlands of Boreray, Berneray, Pabbay, Enſay, and Caillegray, are, for the moſt part, covered with ſhelly-ſand, which, towards the ſhores, is drifted by the winds into great hills. Even in theſe ſmall Iſles, there are freſh-water lakes, full of fiſh.

The Long Iſland, comprehending Lewis and Harris, is in length, from north to ſouth, about 90 miles. Harris the Southern is divided from Lewis the Northern by a tremendous ridge of very high mountains, abounding with deer, which until the game laws were vigourouſly enforced by the proprietor, were conſidered as common property. The whole face of Harris is ſingularly rugged and forbidding, being ſurrounded and interſected with

with rocks, marshes, mountains, hills of shelly sand; and lashed and stunned on the west and north with the tremendous roar of the fierce Atlantic Ocean. In this island there are several fresh-water lakes, as well as considerable rivers, stored with trout and salmon.

The east side of Lewis consists in rocks, mountains, marshes, and lakes, from four miles to ten in length; but from Stornaway by Graish, to the northern extremity, it is, on the whole, though here and there interspersed with hills, both beautiful and fertile. Here the soil is either pure moss, or moss intermixed with sand and earth, or a mixture of sand and earth without any moss. It produces plentiful crops of barley and potatoes, and in some parts, of oats and rye.—This part of Lewis is passable for foot as well as horsemen. But in most places the least vestige of a tract or path is not to be discerned: so that, what little intercourse takes place in this rugged island, is carried on by means of boats, on the rivers, lakes, and morasses when covered by water. Near the coast of Lewis and Harris lie the two Berneras,

neras, compofed of mofs and fand, and feveral fmaller iflands, of the fame kind of foil, as Pabbay-fcarpe, Taranfay, Haifgear, &c. all of them fertile, efpecially, as throughout the whole of the Hebrides, and other countries, when manured with fea vegetables or weeds.

The whole weft fide of Uift, being plain and fandy, is extremely pleafant to ride through; but attended with danger to ftrangers and fuch as are overtaken by liquor; on account of fords over which the fea flows from eaft to weft fo rapidly, and which are at the fame time of fuch extent, that an active horfe or footman will hardly gain the further fide, before the tide has filled up fome one or other of the many fmall hollow channels of rivulets he has to crofs.

Benbecula, or Nun-toun, the feat of Clanronald, becomes an ifland twice in 24 hours: and thofe immenfe fords refemble large feas over which confiderable veffels, at certain feafons, may fail with fafety. The whole of this country is unfavourable to wood of almoft all kinds, which creeps along the earth: as the juniper, thorns, and all kinds of natural

tural brush-wood, mountain-ash, wild vines, hysop, nay, even apple and pear, and plumb trees, with gooseberry and currant bushes, though surrounded by high garden walls, must keep their heads below; and fruits seldom arrive at perfection, though tenderly cultivated and secured from storms.

All kinds of greens or garden roots, used over Britain, are planted in gentlemen's gardens, and some of them with success. In Uist there is a kind of natural kail, or colewort, called *morran*, that grows by the sea-side: with long grass called *bent*, used in making sacks, ropes, and other implements of husbandry. There is also another root called *rue*, that the common people once used for dying woollen yarn red; but strictly prohibited of late, for fear of making a passage for the wind to blow away the sand, and disfigure the face of the fields. A nourishing root is commonly dug up by the poor, in time of scarcity, out of the arable lands, called *brisgean*, or wild sherrat, and when boiled, answers the purpose of bread or potatoes: they are also prohibited from this as much as possible. Digging or opening the lands for these roots

exposes

expofes the field to be blown away by the drift. Here are carmile roots, wild carrots, baldmony, hemlock, heath, rufhes, ftrawberries, black-berries, cranberries, juniperberries, and feveral other wild fruits.

But no broom, whins, or thorns, will thrive here. There are plenty of peats and turf for fire over all the ifles.

The fpecies of land and fea fowls over all this country are too many to be mentioned in fo limited a work as this. Tarmachans, plowers, black-birds, ftarlings (or druiddan) red muir-cocks and hens, ducks and wild geefe, by thoufands, particularly on the plains of South Uift and elfewhere, wood-cocks, fnipes, ravens, carrion crows, herons, bats, owls, all kinds of hawks and eagles, fo large and ftrong, that they carry off lambs, kids, fawns, and the weaker kinds of fheep and foals. They have been known to attack even cows, horfes, and ftags. And their nefts are frequently found to be plentifully fupplied with fifh, which, in what are called plays of fifh, they pick up from the furface of the fea.

A fpecies

A species of robbery, equally singular and cruel, was lately practised in this country very commonly, and sometimes at this day, in which the eagles are the principal actors. The thieves, coming upon the eaglets in their nests, in the absence of their dams, sow up the extremity of the great gut: so that the poor creatures, tortured by obstructions, express their sense of pain in frequent and loud screams. The eagle, imagining their cries to proceed from hunger, is unwearied in the work of bringing in fresh prey, to satisfy, as she thinks, their craving appetites. But all that spoil is carried home by the thieves at night, when they come to give a momentary relief to the eaglet, for the purpose of prolonging, for their own base ends, their miserable existence. This infernal practice is now wearing fast away, being strictly watched by the gentlemen, and severely punished. Mr. Mackenzie, for every eagle killed in Lewis, gives half a crown. One of those large eagles was taken in the Isle of Herries, at Tarbert, together with a large turbot, in which the animal had fastened its talons, when asleep, at the surface of the water, so as not to be able to disengage them.

The eagle, with his large wings expanded like sails, drove before the wind, into the harbour, where he was taken alive; his feet being entangled in the turbot by the country people.

Birds of passage, of several kinds, are seen over all the Isles: swans, cuckoos, swallows, lapwings, plovers, &c. and wild fowls of several kinds, rendered tame, are to be seen about the yards, dunghills, and doors of houses, among the poultry.

The *Bishop Carara*, or *Bunubhuachil*, is larger than any goose, of a brown colour, the inside of the wing white, the bill long and broad. It dives quicker than any other bird. It was never known to fly, the wings being too short to carry a weight seldom under, but often above sixteen pounds.

The *Black Cormorant* is not held in much estimation by the Islanders; but such as have white feathers in their wings, and white down on their bodies, are famous for making soup or broth of a very delicate taste and flavour.

The

The Western Hebrides abound in soland-geese, sea-gulls, and singing-ducks, of a size somewhat less than that of common ducks. They are constantly employed either in diving for sand-eels, which are of a speckled colour like leeches, or in sitting together in flocks, and singing, which is heard at the distance of half a mile, and is accounted very pleasing music.

The duck, called the Crawgiabh, is larger than a Muscovy duck, and almost tame: you may approach very near it before it takes wing; and is frequently kept by gentlemen among their other poultry.

*Rain Goose.* This fowl is always heard, at a great distance, before a storm. It is almost as large as a goose.

*Drillechan, or Water Magpye.* This bird is larger than a land magpie, beautifully speckl'd, with a long, sharp, and strong bill, red as blood. It never swims, but flies from place to place, following the ebb, picking up spout-fish. They are silent during the flow of the tide,

tide, and begin to whiftle the moment it turns.

*Shiltachan.* This kind of fea plover never goes far out at fea, but runs about the fandy coaft, and follows every furge to pick up eels or fpout-fifh. They are fpeckled and fmall, but very long legged. Their pipes are extremely fhrill. They are eatable; though too trifling to be fhot, when much better game is found in fo great plenty.

All gregarious birds, whether great or fmall, commonly found an alarm, in cafe they fee any bird, even of a different fpecies, in danger, from man, otters, feal, or any other animal.

*Starnags.* This bird appears in fpring, on thefe coafts, about the fize of a hawk, with long fharp pointed wings, extremely noify and daring. They are fpeckled, but the prevailing colour is white.

*Fafgatar.* This bird is of blackifh blue, as large as a hawk, and is conftantly purfuing the Starnags through the air, to force them

them to throw out of their mouths whatever they have eaten; and the vile creatures catch every atom of what the others throw out, before it reaches the water. It will ſometimes venture to ſit on any boat, if the paſſengers have proviſions, and throw out any, by way of encouraging its approaches.

*Wild Doves.* Every cave and clift is full of wild doves.

*Sheep.* The ſheep are of various colours, as black, grey, dun, and party-coloured; many of them with four horns.

*Cows, horſes, goats, and deer,* are here in great plenty. Alſo, pole-cats, or metterick. This animal is almoſt as large as a cat, and very deſtructive to the young kids: it cuts their throats, and ſucks the blood. Its bite is hurtful to cows and horſes. The ſkin is as ſmooth as any fur, and of a brown colour.

There are weaſels to be met with, and conies, in different iſlands. Serpents have been dug up in great cluſters, quite benumbed and

and seemingly dead, in winter, particularly in Harris: few people, however, have suffered from their bites.

There are no *foxes, moles,* or *hares,* over all the Long Isle; nor *ferrets, partridges, black-cocks,* nor many of the granavirous fowls; a strong proof that grain has not been long sown here, and that the country has not been so thoroughly cultivated, as to entice them to reside in it.

*Otters and Seals* are swarming over the whole coast, and their skins and oil bring the merchants considerable profits at market.

The fish commonly used by the inhabitants are the *cuddies,* which are almost as thick on the east coasts, as the herring fry is, in their season. These are taken by hundreds, at one dipping of a bag-net, called Tabh, made for the purpose, *i. e.* a large hoop bound to the end of a long pole, with a pock net bound to it. The fisher throws out of his mouth fragments of boiled limpets, over the surface, where the net lies.

Shoals

Shoals of cuddies leap upon the bait, regardlefs of their danger, when the net is gradually raifed above the water, and about them. The fecond year, this fifh is twelve inches long. The third, they are larger ftill, and known by the name of Saiths. The fourth year they are called Uxes, and equal the falmon in bulk and in ftrength. Around thefe are plenty of lyths, cods, herrings, fmall and great ling, falmon, and trout, in Harris; but particularly in Lewis, where there are fo many large and fmall rivers and lochs for their reception, from the one end of the country to the other. Likewife, fand-eels, lobfters, crabs, clam-fhell, or fcollops; oyfters, wilks, periwinkles, cockles, muffels, limpets, fpout-fifh, leaving the furface of the fand full of their dung in little heaps; barnacles, faftened to rocks, and large logs of wood, with more kinds of fhell-fifh, that might be mentioned.

*Dog-fifh.* There are fwarms of dog-fifh, fcates, blind-fifh, and the firft place in Britain for herrings and large whales, bafking or fun fifh, turbots, mackerels, cat-fifh, &c.

However unfavourable this country is to the growth of wood at prefent, it is evident, that there was once great plenty of it all over the iflands: for the roots and trunks of large trees are found in deep moffes, bearing unequivocal impreffions of fire; which make the people fay, that the Norwegians burnt the wood when they were obliged to retreat from the Scottifh iflands and fea-coafts to their native Scandinavia.

On the eaft fide of that vaft ridge of iflands, which is the fubject of thefe notes, and on the weft too of Lewis, though not of the Uifts and Barray, there are a great many fafe and fpacious harbours, fome of them large enough to receive the greateft fleets; as Loch Erifka, Loch Boifdale, Loch Maddy, Loch Finfbay, Loch Tarbet, Loch Sea-forth, Birkin Ifles, Loch Stornoway: and on the weft fide of the Long Ifle, Loch Rogue, Loch Carlovay, Loch Reafort, and Loch Leofoway, &c. Thefe lochs are moft happily fituated for receiving the herrings, when driven towards the coaft for fhelter from ftorms. Shoals of them are catched
here

here by the country people. As to the herring buſſes, they commonly remain on the eaſt ſide of Lewis, or on the coaſt of Scotland. But the moſt advantageous ſtations for fiſhings are, beyond all doubt, to be found on the weſtern ſide of the Weſtern Hebrides.

CHAP.

## CHAP. II.

*The political State of the Western Hebrides—The principal Proprietors—Tacksmen—Sub-tenants—Predial Slaves, or Scallags.*

THE first landholder towards the southern extremity of this extensive ridge of Islands, is Macneil, laird over all Barray, as well as the lesser adjoining islands. Mr. Macneil generally resides on his estate, an extensive property, which he manages with equal humanity and prudence. He encourages all kinds of improvement, exercises justice among his tenants, and protects them from those oppressions, which are too common in other parts of the Hebrides. This gentleman has few or no tacksmen, except some of his own near relations, who are of too gentle and generous a disposition to abuse the confidence placed in them by their chief, by trampling on a poor, but kindred people. The minister of Barray has but

but a small farm, in comparison of those possessed by many other clergymen in the Hebrides, who, like some other tacksmen, are too prone to treat their sub-tenants with great severity; examples of which we shall see by and by.

Mr. Macdonald of Boisdale, a great landholder, and a most honourable gentleman, seldom leaves South Uist, except on a visit to the capital, or to look after his estates in other countries. He is universally allowed to be the best farmer in the west of Scotland. He lays plans of rural œconomy before his tenants, and, by his own example, leads them, as it were, by the hand, to execute them for their own benefit. He distributes justice, and preserves peace and order among his people, like a prudent and kind master of a family, whom his houshold both love and esteem. The next landholder, as we advance north-ward in South Uist, is

Mr. Macdonald of Clanronald; or, as he is oftener called Clanronald, and oftener still by that of CLAN. Clan has a large estate in South Uist, besides that in Scotland,
with

with Cannay, and other iflands. This gentleman's family fucceeded to the gallant Allan Macdonald, who loft his life in the battle of Sheriff Muir, between Crieff and Stirling, in the year 1715. The prefent Clan has made what is called the grand tour of Europe, is fenfible and fprightly in his converfation, and endowed with a tolerable fhare of knowledge: but a fet of interefted and artful men, operating on his difpofition to conviviality and facility of temper, have unfortunately led him to turn feveral hundreds of fouls (the defcendants of thofe kinfmen who followed his anceftors, their chief, with enthufiafm, into the field of battle) out of their poffeffions, and beftowed their farms, by large tracts of country, on a few favourites.

The people turned out of Clanronald's eftates were fubftantial farmers, whofe fpirits were not crufhed by extreme poverty, and who, having the means of tranfporting themfelves and their families to other countries, fcorned either to truckle to the favourite tackfman, or to live longer in a land, in which their children, if not themfelves,

felves, muſt, ſooner or later, fall into the humiliating condition of ſcallags.---There is a notion common, not only among the common people, but alſo among thoſe whoſe property and rank give them ſome influence in the government, that it is only the pooreſt of the people that emigrate; on which account, they think, that emigrations are the leſs to be regretted. They are under a great miſtake. It is only people of ſome property, and that not inconſiderable, who can afford to tranſport themſelves and their families to diſtant countries. Of

North Uiſt, the ſole proprietor is Lord Macdonald, who is alſo proprietor of more than half the Iſle of Skye. His eſtate in Skye is of vaſt extent, and abounds in all the neceſſaries of life. His Lordſhip has reverſed the œconomy of his kinſman, Clanronald; for, inſtead of diſmiſſing the actual cultivators of the land, he has taken them under his own immediate protection, and ſettled them by dozens, in the room of one overgrown land-broker, or tackſman. Yet it is juſtice to mention, that Lord Macdonald did not expel the tackſmen, but only reduced

reduced their immoderate farms. His Lordship has been subjected to much unmerited obloquy. His tenants, according to their station, and in comparison of the sub-tenants of tacksmen, live in a state of affluence. It is also to be observed, that although, on the whole, his Lordship chuses to multiply industrious and contented husbandmen, rather than to support idle gentlemen, he has been known, in the choice of tenants, to give a preference to gentlemen of active turns already settled on his estate, before others, who made larger and more tempting offers for their farms. He is very attentive to the equal and prompt distribution of justice among his tenants.

The estate of Harris belongs to Mr. Macleod, at present in India. His father, Alexander Macleod, made a purchase of it from the chief of that name. That gentleman, Alex. Macleod, resided at Roudle for some years, and spent much time and money in making piers and harbours at that place, where vessels might be stationed in safety. He repaired old churches, built new houses and repaired old ones: he brought wheels, reels,

reels, and other implements, to begin a woollen manufactory in his village: he alſo encouraged a great many artificers; as ſhoemakers, weavers, turners, and wrights, and maſons. He was alſo at much pains to begin roads through the country, as the firſt ſtep towards improvements in any country like this, that lies in a ſtate of nature, and diſcovered a ſincere deſire of encouraging induſtry among the poor people, whom he greatly pitied for their depreſſed and naked appearance; and whom he found not only neglected, but wantonly abuſed and inſulted.

He made a tour around the whole back parts of his extenſive eſtate, and even entered the huts of the tenants, and declared openly that the wigwams of the wild Indians of America were equally good, and better furniſhed. This gentleman was ſincerely intereſted for the good of his people. But, after a generous ſtruggle, for years, to bring about a regular plan of improvement among them, he found himſelf fighting againſt the ſtream; for the tackſmen counteracted his well intended ſchemes, as they underſtood, that the more they co-operated with him,

the

the sooner their own weight in the scale would be lessened; because all his endeavours pointed towards emancipating the enslaved tenantry, which, in the end, would utterly overthrow their established system of passive obedience among the inferior class of men in all this country. That their own importance might not therefore be diminished in the end, they seldom supported him but with reluctance, only to save appearances; so that he was known to say, before he gave up the regular system of animating the poor tenantry, that his spirits were hurt at the concealed opposition made to his well meant intentions of laying new resources open to the industrious poor, to exercise their talents, for bettering their circumstances.

But if the poor sub-tenants of Herries found little relief or consolation from the presence and benignant efforts of their good and respectable landlord, what have they to expect now that he is no more, and his successor at a distance? Nothing, surely, but additional oppression, heavier and more intolerable. While he was present they
durst

durst not act very outrageously, for they stood in some awe. Though they knew that he could not force them to relax during the run of their lease, yet there was a kind of forced reserve put on all their external actions; which, since his departure, is quite laid aside, and the case of the poor sufferers is more deplorable.

Mr. Alexander Macleod, by speaking familiarly to the poor, found out the secrets of the rich, and was astonished at the result. Had his predecessor taken this prudent step, it is thought he might have made his fortune at Dunvegan, without visiting the Indies; and continued proprietor of a country 36 miles in length, with the richest islands on earth in proportion to their extent, kelp and cattle included, with the valuable Isle of St. Kilda; and also have protected 3,000 souls from the infamous oppression under which most of them are now groaning.

Mackenzie of Seaforth is the sole proprietor of all Lewis, a tract of country of, or about seventy miles in length, and twenty miles in breadth, with many fertile islands adjacent.

adjacent. All Lewis is inhabited, for the most part by tenants, who rent their farms immediately from himself. Mr. Mackenzie easily perceived the folly, as well as the inhumanity, of lending out the people on his island to imperious tackfmen, for the purpose of raising fortunes to themselves on the ruins of the unfortunate subtenants. The greatest tackfman in Lewis is the laird's ground officer; a place of great power and trust as well as emolument, in districts where the will of the landholder, or that of his agent, is of greater efficacy than written laws or records. The station he holds is a pledge for his good behaviour, in the character of tackfman; for should he commit any confiderable act of violence or injustice to his inferior cottagers, he would foon be removed from his master's good graces, and from his office.

The British laws have been introduced by Mr. Mackenzie into Lewis. In the town of Stornoway there are magistrates, who regularly sit in judgment to hear and decide the different controversies that are brought before them, by passing sentence impartially every week: besides this, the Sheriff-Depute,

pute holds courts in that town, as do alſo the Juſtice of the Peace and Baron Bailie.

Mr. Mackenzie has a noble preſence, and handſome open countenance. He may well ſeem to be the head of a great clan. He has excellent parts and univerſal knowledge, but is particularly diſtinguiſhed by his enthuſiaſm and attainments in natural hiſtory. Though he is deaf from an early misfortune, he is very lively and pleaſing in converſation. The company ſpell the words on their fingers, and Mackenzie anſwers by ſpeech. Being extremely quick of apprehenſion, he will carry on a regular diſcourſe on any ſubject with his gueſts. After ſeeing a few letters ſpelt on the fingers, he immediately ſupplies the reſt, and ſaves them the trouble of going through the whole.

Thoſe who have the honour of viſiting at his houſe, are at pains to touch their fingers cleverly; and moſt of the gentlemen at Stornaway are adepts at this kind of learning, in order to make themſelves underſtood and agreeable, while in company: and I have been much delighted to ſee and hear them converſe

converse, the one by the fingers and figns, and the other by fpeech.

Mackenzie has brought to Harris, partridges, and other animals, formerly unknown in Lewis, from the main land, to raife a breed there for game: he is an excellent fhot himfelf, and delights much in fowling and hunting, and other manly fports and diverfions.

The prefent Mackenzie, head and reprefentative of the Mackenzies of Seaforth, fucceeded to his brother, Colonel Mackenzie Humberftone, who loft his life in the war in India, that terminated in 1783. General Macleod, Colonel Humberftone, and fome other officers, had left the army at Bednore, and came ftraight to Bombay, in order to lay before the Council the mad conduct and unheard-of rapacity and injuftice of General Matthews. On their return in the Ranger Snow to join the army, of which General Macleod was now appointed Commander in Chief, on the 8th of April, 1783, off Geriah, they fell in with the Maratta fleet of five fail of fquare-rigged veflels.—

Notwithftanding

Notwithstanding this excessive disparity of force, the Captain of the Ranger refused to strike to the enemy. An obstinate battle ensued: nor did it cease till almost every man in the English ship was killed or wounded. Among the former was Major Shaw of the hundredth regiment; and among the latter, Brigadier General Macleod, Colonel Mackenzie Humberstone, and Lieutenant John Taylor; who, together with the Captain of the ship, Pruin, and other prisoners, were carried into Geriah, a port of the Marattas, where they remained for several weeks. Colonel Humberstone died of his wounds, in the twenty-eighth year of his age. General Macleod recovered, being wounded but slightly: so also did Captain Taylor, though severely wounded, and that two gun balls went through and through different parts of his body: he even recovered soon, enjoying a sound and excellent constitution, and in the character of a brave officer, as well as commissary to the army, at a time when the company's finances and credit were at the lowest ebb, by his personal credit, activity, and address, rendered the most essential service to the company and to his

his country. The writer of THE MEMOIRS OF THE LATE WAR IN ASIA, from which I have taken thefe anecdotes, makes the following brief eulogium on Colonel Mackenzie Humberftone. " An early and habitual converfancy with the heroes of ancient as well as modern times, nourifhed in his mind a paffion for military glory, and fupported him, under remitting application, to all thofe ftudies by which he might improve his mind, rife to honourable diftinction, and render his name immortal. He was not only acute, but profound and fteady in his views, gallant without oftentation and fpirited without temerity and imprudence." Two great chiefs from the Hyperborean Iflands of the Hebrides, making war on the fhores of India, prefent a picture of the prefent extended intercourfe among nations, and of the natural fway that hardy have over effeminate climates.

Thefe then are the principal landholders in the Weftern Hebrides.

The TACKSMEN who rent from the great proprietors of land large diftricts, are able

in

in general to rank with gentlemen of from 2 or 300l. to 1,000l. and upwards a year. They are, for the moſt part, relations of the families of whom they hold their leaſes; and many of them half-pay officers of the army. Miniſters too of pariſhes have, for the moſt part, advantageous leaſes, of which they make much greater account than of their ſtipends. There are ſome of the tackſmen who unite the buſineſs of grazing and agriculture with that of trade, and oftener of ſmuggling. There is not perhaps any part of the world where the good things of this life are more unequally diſtributed. While the ſcallag and ſubtenant are wholly at the mercy of the tackſman, the tackſman, from a large and advantageous farm, the cheapneſs of every neceſſary, and by means of ſmuggling of every luxury, rolls in eaſe and affluence.

In South Uiſt the chief tackſmen are, Captain Macdonald, tackſman of Phroboſt, ſon and ſucceſſor to the laird of Boiſdale, whoſe good qualities he inherits, and particularly a tender concern for the comfort of his subtenants and scallags; the minister of Howmore, who has accumulated several farms on the expulsion and ruin of the former possessor; the tacksmen of Milton, Geary, Vailteas, Staal Gheary, and Borenish-wachir; and Mr. Patrick Nicholson, an industrious farmer and enterprizing merchant. Mr. Nicholson, in his commerce with mankind, is as just and upright as any man in his line of life, and in a quarter so distant from the seats of law and government, can well be supposed to be. He is a great encourager of the industrious poor; and, though not a native of the place, is highly and justly esteemed by all ranks of people.

In North Uist, Mr. Macdonald Balranald, a very sensible and agreeable man, has greatly improved his farm, by draining lochs, and converting the ground into rich arable fields. It is to be hoped that his landlord, who, through his well-directed industry, will acquire a considerable accession to his landed property will reward him, at the expiration of his present lease, according to his merit.

Another

Another valuable farm in North Uift is poffeffed by the reverend gentleman of Ty-Geary; who of all the tackfmen, clergymen, and gentlemen of the Weftern Ifles of Scotland, is the largeft and jollieft, as well as one of the moft hofpitable and the beft natured. Never was the minifter and tackfman of Ty-Gheary known to kick, beat, or fcourge, or, in any fhape, to lift his hand againft his fcallags in the whole courfe of his life. Were he not fo well tempered a man, this moderation, not a little unufual in the Weftern Hebrides, might be afcribed to motives of felf-intereft; for a few blows, even with his naked fift, would break their bones to pieces, and render them for ever ufelefs to himfelf or to others.

Mr. Macdonald, Balifhear, is factor and baron bailie on Lord Macdonald's eftate in this ifland; an office which places him above the neceffity, as a focial and convivial turn renders him fuperior to an inclination towards thofe fordid arts too often practifed by tackfmen. Lord Macdonald, in what is called the laft fet, that is, the laft renewal of his leafes in North Uift, has laid a pretty heavy

heavy hand on Mr. Maclean, tackſman of Heiſgear; Mr. Macdonald, tackſman of Trumpis Geary; and Mr. Maclean of Solas. But as all of theſe gentlemen have thought proper to become old batchelors, it is charitably to be preſumed, that his Lordſhip meant this as a gentle rebuke for their neglect of matrimony.

Another tackſman in North Uiſt, not to be paſſed over in ſilence, is Captain Macdonald of Valay; a gentleman ſtrictly honourable, without hauteur and pride, complaiſant without deceit; humble, yet commanding reſpect; hoſpitable, without vanity or oſtentation; chearful, yet equally free from all indecency and affectation; charitable to the poor, beloved and eſteemed by all.

Mr. Maclean of Bournay is raither a laird than a tackſman, as he derives immenſe wealth from the quantities of kelp manufactured on his iſland; and as his leaſe continues for generations to come.

The iſland of Harris, thirty-ſix miles in length, and from five to fourteen in breadth,

breadth, with a number of inferior and adjacent ifles, the whole upwards of twelve miles in circumference, is divided among five great tackfmen.

Harris, with its dependent ifles, contains about three thoufand fouls, moft of them in a ftate of actual bondage. Mr. Norman Macleod, tackfman of Bernera, when we confider the vaft number of his fubtenants, fervants, and fcallags; the farms, with cowhoufes, &c. in his own hand, and the kelp made on his numerous rocks and ifles, may be reckoned the firft tackfman in the ifles, or in North Britain. This gentleman and his lady are both advanced in years. They have three daughters, all of whom will, at the death of their father, be well provided for. Mr. Macleod has introduced into his diftrict many new improvements; as Englifh fheep, and large horfes and bulls to mend the breed of cattle; as alfo jack-affes to breed mules, a hardy kind of animal, and well fitted for labour in a hilly and rugged country. He fows peas, turnips, and lintfeed, to advantage. He has introduced the ufe of carts and fledges into his hufbandry,

inftead

inftead of carriage on the backs of horfes and fcallags; and mills wrought by horfes, inftead of the hand-mill or quern. He fets many good examples to his neighbours and tenants, and is, on the whole, a ufeful and refpectable member of fociety. But he gives himfelf no trouble about the execution of juftice: he leaves the other tackfmen to treat their fubtenants and cottagers with all the freedom and caprice of a Scottifh baron before the jurifdiction act.

The tackfman of Enfay is factor for all the eftate of Harris. He is alfo baron bailie, though he has not held a court for thefe feven years. He deals deeply in the kelp trade, and alfo in illicit trade.

The tackfman of Strond is diftinguifhed by humanity to his fubtenants and fcallags, who are objects of envy to all the other fubtenants and fcallags in Harris.

The man who now enjoys the leafe of St. Kilda, being lame and decrepit, was for fometime a charity fchoolmafter in that place ---Of whom afterwards, when treating of St. Kilda.

The population of Harris is eſtimated at three thouſand ſouls; moſt of whom, except the few who rent their farms immediately from the laird, are as obedient to the nod of the five great tackſmen, or captains, as ever their forefathers were to their warlike chiefs, when the *croſh tarridh*, or war ſignal, was lighted.

The gentlemen in the Weſtern Iſlands have, many of them, the advantage of an univerſity education. They are commonly connected together by the ties of matrimony, or conſanguinity, or otherwiſe, which makes them firm to one another; while the commoners are no leſs united among themſelves, by ſimilar bonds of friendſhip, in their reſpective departments.

The oldeſt ſon generally ſucceeds to the tack, a much better birth than any of the other ſons find, unleſs ſome extraordinary good fortune falls in the way of ſuch as go in queſt of bread to other countries.

The young ladies are generally worſe off, being obliged to form ſuch connections as

remain

remain in the country, or continue single, in case the gentleman is not agreeable to her, after making his addresses; for their own equals in point of rank are commonly sent abroad, either in the army or navy, or some other line of bread.

CHAP.

## CHAP. III.

*Tackſmen — Subtenants — Scallags — Predial Slaves.*

THE ſame ingenious and patriotic traveller, whom I have already mentioned,* in his Tour in England and Scotland, replete with uſeful inſtruction as well as elegant entertainment, in a comparative view, which he takes of the former and the preſent ſtate of the Highlands of Scotland, makes the following juſt and intereſting obſervations.

" The actual ſyſtem of landed property in the weſt of Europe has varied its form with the prevailing character of ſucceſſive ages. It has been accommodated to the rude ſimplicity of the more antient times, as well as to the feudal chivalry of the middle ages. In the preſent times, it is every where

\* Captain Newte.

where subjected to a new modification, from the genius and maxims of a commercial age, and from increasing industry and cultivation. But, from this modification, flagrant oppressions have arisen; the lordly chief applying the maxims of an age in which money is the universal representative, and letters the universal media of transferring property, to establishments founded in times when the great proprietors of land, wholly employed in hunting, military exploits, and rude conviviality, never dreamed of increasing their fortunes by means of commerce: which, if they had known, they would have disdained. The glory of the chief was the glory of all his kindred and name: and the numbers and fidelity of his vassals and tenants, again, were what constituted the power and consequence of the chief. The produce of land, corn, cattle, fish, and game, were spent on the estate, but chiefly at the mansion-houses of the great, in generous hospitality. And in those times, the Highlanders were better fed, and, in general, finer men than they are at present. For now the cattle, the salmon, and the very game, are either carried or driven out of the country:

nor

nor has the faint dawn of commerce been yet able to fupply that abundance which preceded it."

This Englifh gentleman could not have given a more a faithful account of thefe things, if he had lived in the Highland countries for a long feries of years. When the great landholders lived among the hufbandmen, who were for the moft part allied to them by blood, or at leaft the famenefs of name, the people loved their chiefs: and each laird and lord was accounted rich or poor according to the number of tenants that poffeffed their lands. But now, in the abfence of the great proprietors, the power and influence of the laird is transferred to a few tackfmen; who, in fome inftances, of late, squeeze them without mercy. The tackfmen and fubtenants, formerly, or nearly, on an equal footing, were wont to plead their caufe, on equal terms, before a common chief. At prefent they are obliged to be much more fubmiffive to their tackfmen than ever they were, in former times, to their lairds or lords. Formerly, they were a free, animated, and bold people, commanding refpect from their undaunted,

courage

courage, and repelling injuries from whatever quarter they came, both by words and actions. But, now they muſt approach even the tackſmen with cringing humility, heartleſs, and diſcouraged, with tattered rags, hungry bellies, and down-caſt looks, carrying their own implements of huſbandry for ten or twelve miles back and forward, over hills and mountains, to do the work of their tackſmen: and muſt either ſit wet in their cloaths all night in a dirty kitchen, or ſleep in dirty cloaths, particularly at Luſkintire in Harris, expoſed to be trampled on by ſwine, where the kitchen is commonly the ſtye. But I muſt here obſerve, that there is a great difference between that mild treatment which is ſhewn to ſubtenants and even ſcallags, by the old leſſees, deſcended of ancient and honourable families, and the outrageous rapacity of thoſe neceſſitous ſtrangers, who have obtained leaſes from abſent proprietors, who treat the natives as if they were a conquered, and inferior race of mortals. Formerly, a Highlander would have drawn his dirk againſt even a laird, if he had ſubjected him to the indignity of a blow: at preſent, any tyrannical tackſman, in the abſence of the laird or lord,

lord, whose presence alone can enforce good order and justice, may strike a scallag, and even a subtenant, with perfect impunity. What a degree of spirit and virtue is to be expected from a people so humbled, so enslaved? What degree of courage, or even inclination to repel an invading enemy? " If we have not much money," some of these tacksmen have been known to say, " we have men enough: let us wear them well while they are in our power." In short, they treat them like beasts of burthen; and in all respects like slaves attached to the soil, as they cannot obtain new habitations, on account of the combinations already mentioned, and are entirely at the mercy of the laird or tacksman. I agree entirely with those gentlemen who contend for the breaking of entails, and limiting and restraining excessive farms, on the ground of a wise and humane œconomy? May we not go a step farther, and enquire, if the expulsion of tenantry whose fathers have held their farms, perhaps for ages, be strictly legal, even according to our present laws? If this be agreeable to law, it is not certainly consonant with the genius of the British constitution; nor indeed of any political conftitution: for if it were, it would be in the power of a great chief, or a confederacy of chiefs, to depopulate whole iflands, and other territories, and thereby weaken and even annihilate the ftrength and fecurity of the nation. A rife in rent, proportionate to the rifing price of labour and provifions, that is, the gradual depreciation of the value of money, would be right: as is the cafe, in the perpetual leafes granted, of late, by the crown, and certain territorial lords in Denmark. But no violent and fudden extermination! The load of fuffering has been gradually preffed heavier and heavier down upon the immediate cultivators of land in the iflands, and more remote parts of the Highlands, from feudal times, when the heart and the fword of a tenant was deemed the nobleft and the fureft treafure, to the prefent.

Formerly, the perfonal fervice of the tenant did not, ufually, exceed eight or ten days in the year. There lives, at prefent, at Scalpa, in the Ifle of Harris, a tackfman of a large diftrict, who inftead of fix days work

work paid by the subtenants to his predecessor in the lease, has raised the predial service, called in that and in other parts of Scotland, *manerial bondage*, to fifty-two days in the year at once; besides many other services to be performed at different though regular and stated times: as tanning leather for brogues; making heather ropes for thatch; digging and drying peats for fewel; one pannier of peat charcoal to be carried to the smith; so many days for gathering and shearing sheep and lambs; for ferrying cattle from island to island, and other distant places; and several days for going on distant errands; so many pounds of wool to be spun into yarn. And over and above all this, they must lend their aid, upon any unforeseen occurrence, whenever they are called on. The constant service of two months at once is performed, at the proper season, in the making of kelp. On the whole, this gentleman's subtenants may be computed to devote to his service full three days in the week. But this is not all: they have to pay, besides, yearly, a certain number of cocks, hens, butter, and cheese, called CAORIGH-FERRIN, the WIFE'S PORTION! This, it must be owned, is one of

the

the moſt ſevere and rigorous tackſmen deſcended from the old inhabitants, in all the Weſtern Hebrides: but the ſituation of his ſubtenants exhibits but too faithful a picture of the ſubtenants of thoſe places in general; and the exact counterpart of ſuch enormous oppreſſion is to be found at Luſkintire.

This man was bred, like many of his countrymen, for the ſea-ſervice, and underwent many viciſſitudes of fortune both by ſea and land. He was ſhipwrecked, taken priſoner by the French, eſcaped almoſt naked, ſtruggled with many difficulties for years in America, and afterwards came home to the iſles, and dealt in ſpirits, ſugar, tea, coffee, and the kelp trade; by all which means he amaſſed a conſiderable fortune. Thus rich, and independent, this man, it is ſaid, took his father's leaſe over his head. The old man and his wife, ſtung with vexation and grief, rather than live in ſome adjoining hut at the mercy of ſuch a ſon, went with the reſt of their family to America, where the aged parents of this unnatural child died ſoon after in wretched poverty.

He afterwards turned out of his large and fine farm, the whole of his relations, who held little poſſeſſions on it, and who fell ſoon into great want.

There is a ſpecies of tenantry ſtill in the Weſtern Hebrides, as heretofore throughout Scotland, who hold their poſſeſſions by a kind of tenure called *Steel-Bow*; or, the appraiſement of the whole ſtock of cattle, houſes, and implements of huſbandry, and every thing elſe belonging to the farm, on condition of the tenants' paying a certain yearly rent, and, at the expiration of the leaſe, leaving the premiſes exactly as he found them. This is the caſe of Luſkintire at preſent.

The poor Hebrideans are on foot every morning at five o'clock at lateſt: the women at their querns or hand-mills: the men at ſome other piece of employment until day-light invites them into the field, or to the ſea ſhores, where they muſt begin a ſet taſk of cutting ſea-weed with the ebbing of the tide. They are obliged to work as for life or death, that they may be able to get their quantity of ſea-weed carried clear off.

If when they are on work for their Master, whether laird or tackſman, they ſhould be an hour behind the time fixed for their making their appearance, they are inſtantly trounced home, with orders to be there more early the next morning. No apology will be admitted: neither the inclemency of the weather, nor the height nor ruggedneſs of the hills they had to croſs, nor an accident by the road, nor the loſs of that day, to thoſe who have ſo few they can call their own, very precious. All goes for nothing. The intereſt, the will of the maſter muſt be attended to, not theirs. To all this ſeverity the unfeeling tackſman often adds cruel mockings and imprecations.

This treatment, bad as it is, might be borne by a people whoſe ſpirits are ſubdued by unremitting, unalleviated inſolence and oppreſſion. But the maſter, or his overſeer, called a *grieve*, often, on the moſt frivolous pretences, abandons himſelf to burſts of paſſion, and with hands, feet, and rods, breaks the bones of men and women too. This is not an exaggerated picture. The broken ribs of one young maid, named Maclellan, from the village

village of Cluor, atteft the fact; which was committed by a tackfman affuming the title of Doctor. The fame Doctor (reverfed) almoft took the life of another innocent maid, from Shileboft; though fhe gave no other offence than that of tarrying a little longer than he wifhed, at her miftrefs's defire, to finifh fomething fhe had in hands. This girl was fo bruifed, that the Doctor was obliged to lock her up from her parents for fome days, left, by feeing her danger, their feelings might be raifed above the dread of the tyrant, and they fhould fly for vengeance with the cry of murder in their mouths, to the Doctor's landlord, Captain Macleod, who, it was faid, had the young woman died, would not have interfered to fave his tenant, but have fuffered the law to take its courfe. Though fhe will never again be perfectly well or able to bear fatigue, fhe fo far recovered her ftrength as to bear the ftrefs of being carried to her father's houfe.

" The Celts," fays Mr. Pinkerton, in his Hiftory of the Picts, " had, and ftill have, a natural contempt for the fair fex; for, being mere favages, but one degree above brutes,

brutes, they remain still in much the same state of society as in the days of Julius. The Samoeids are remarkable for the same contempt of their women, whom they regard as impure; and treat their wives with the utmost tyranny and brutality. Whoever travels among them will see these savages stretched at their ease, and their wives and women toiling like the brute beasts for their unmanly husbands."

One would imagine, that this historian saw the beastly brutality of this action, and the perpetrator lolling in bed, on a cold frosty morning, and pampering his belly with fat cream and butter-milk, until he thought proper to rise by eleven o'clock, to call in his starving wife from winnowing corn, or graddan from the quern, either in a cold barn, or open field, where she stands from day-light, as overseer of the working people, to eat porridge and milk, as tea is too great a luxury for common fare. But the public may believe me, in telling, that few gentlemen over all the isle love their wives like this man, but quite the reverse. I appeal to every traveller of honour and
candour,

candour, who not only has experienced their uncommon hospitality, but has seen the warmth of their affections to their wives. There are no people without some exceptionable characters---Why blame the whole Celts more than others for having a few of that order of mortals among them?

In the Western Hebrides, remote from the springs of government, and almost wholly under the authority of caprice, men of low birth and education, creeping into leases, being of gross, untutored natures, and pampered too with rich and stimulating aliments, indulge themselves in excesses of passion and brutality that, in more refined and better regulated countries, would not, on any account, be tolerated. The tyrant, of whom I have just been speaking, unless he be answered immediately at a call, sets up a horrid growl, which is instantly heard over the whole house, accompanied by threats, very soon and summarily executed. If nobody comes in his way on whom he may wreak his vengeance, he falls with great fury on the furniture of the house, which he hurls against the walls, and breaks into pieces.

He

He is particularly ſtudious, and with great deliberation, ſets about the demolition of whatever article he ſuppoſes a particular value is ſet on by his wife.

I was witneſs of an action that ſtruck me very forcibly at the time when it happened, and which I cannot now recollect without a degree of horror. A man calling himſelf a gentleman, had a mind to horſewhip one of his ſcallags, who had given him ſome offence. But, miſſing the immediate object of his reſentment, he fell in with his ſiſter, a pretty and innocent young damſel, who happened to be carrying a barley cake for her brother's breakfaſt. The gentleman buffeted the girl ſeverely, toſſed the cake out of her hands, and kicked her before him, as ſhe attempted to recover the cake, with his foot.

The gentleman whoſe character I mean to illuſtrate by the above anecdote, has revived an old country ſtatute, entitling the tackſman to any ſheep or lamb that ſhould be found unmarked among his flock, at the time of ſhearing. This regulation, or decree,

cree, or whatever it may be called, was made for the purpofe of preventing thieves from ftealing fheep, under pretence of feeking their own among the tackfman's fheep; but it was either never rigoroufly enforced, or it had fallen into difuetude, and was only held over their heads, *in terrorem*, until this harpy took into his head to carry it into execution. I was told a laughable fquabble that happened between this man and one of his poor fubtenant's wives that lived at a paltry place near Diraclet, called Ceandibeg. This woman had a ftrong fheep that fhe could not catch, for want of a dog bred for that purpofe, as is the cuftom in the ifland, fo that the lamb was not marked when the tackfman collected his fheep. The tackfman feeing a large and fat lamb following the poor man's ewe, ordered one of his fcallags to carry it home for his dinner. But the poor man's wife to whom the lamb belonged, happening to be prefent, remonftrated ftoutly againft fuch an act of injuftice, urging, that the dam that the lamb followed, and by which it was fuckled, fufficiently proved it to be her property. But the tackfman, deaf to all her arguments, re-
                                                newed

newed his orders to his scallags to carry off the lamb. But the fellows knowing the virago they had to deal with, were rather backward to carry their master's orders into execution. Xantippe held better than the tacksman could draw, crying out in the Gâlic language, " Sfear cumal cailliach no taruing bodaich:" that is, " An old woman holds better than an old man can pull." She held the lamb as firmly as a cat holds a mouse: and, after a long struggle, the tacksman of Luskintire was obliged to give up his expected prey, and yield to substantial justice.

It has been alledged, but without any proofs, that he calculates, to a few months, the time when he can become master of the effects of the poor subtenants on his lease, and is always on the look out for a rich one to supply the vacancy, that he may add the man who failed to the number of his scallags. And one Malcolm Macdonald, though turned out of his farm by his master, for political reasons not to be mentioned, preferred keeping by the forest with his cattle for two seasons, however hard, in expectation

tion of meeting with a vacancy in the lands of fome other more humane tackfman, to the acceptance of any farm belonging to this oppreffor, though repeatedly folicited by him to do fo, knowing too well that his effects, more than any perfonal regard for his intereft, were the motives by which this man was influenced. But few or none will come to his lands but fuch as are turned out by other milder tackfmen for fome fault, and have no other place to put their heads in. Of this number he has already, on his ground, upwards of feven families: and among others, a certain well-known man with a number of different wives, and their brood; which is ftill increafing; and likely to add, more and more, to the population of the country.— He is not only a great oppreffor of his poor fubtenants and fcallags, but offenfive to his equals, by the fupercilious infolence and fcoffingnefs of his manners; infomuch that the tackfman of Strond, though the fimpleft man in all the country, was provoked to belabour him with a cudgel. Nay, he was even thrafhed heartily by a ftout fellow, one of his own fcallags. He is alfo a great profaner of the fabbath, forcing his poor fubtenants to

carry

carry burthens on that day, for want of time
to repair to their families on the Saturdays,
and a reviler and mocker of sacred characters.
The sneering severity of his scoffings
against the present minister of St. Kilda made
that reverend man say, that he was an enemy
to mankind; if not in power to resent
it. But it were well if his injurious treatment
of the clergy were confined to banter
and derision: instances are not wanting of
his marking them out as objects of more serious
aggression. A certain clergyman who
had not any house of his own, and who was
under the necessity of wandering from place
to place for quarters in this shamefully neglected
country, yielded, contrary to the advice
of his friends, to the pressing invitations
of the steel-bowman of Luskintire, to become
a preceptor to his children, a lodger and
inmate of his house. But his treatment of
the clergyman was so contrary to the laws
of friendship and honour, that it is soon to
be made a subject of prosecution in a court of
justice. But, in vindication of that noble
spirit of hospitality, good faith, and generosity
toward strangers, which formerly distinguished,
and still in some measure distin-
guishes

guishes the Islands and Highlands of Scotland in general.

I shall relate a fact which happened under the roof of a gentleman of genuine honour, of the name of Campbell, and in this very neighbourhood, to the unfortunate CHARLES STUART, while concealed in the Hebrides, when both the hospitality and secrecy of the honest islanders to that unhappy Prince reflected much honour upon their tender generosity.

As the fact is hitherto unknown to the world, and points out the integrity of the gentleman who afforded the misguided Chevalier the full extent of the laws of hospitality in his distress, I flatter myself the whole of this transaction will not, at this distance of time, be offensive to any person of generosity. It is a fact attested by many living witnesses, that the Prince, with a select band of active gentlemen doubly armed, landed at the Island of Glass, in the Long Isle, before day, on the third morning after the battle of Culloden was fought and gained ed by the Duke of Cumberland. That Prince and his men were concealed for weeks, by Mr. Campbell, until a safe paſſage could be found to carry him to the northern coaſt, where he might paſs through Germany for France. A paſſage was actually beſpoken for that purpoſe, though for political reaſons the promiſed veſſel was afterwards refuſed. Mean time let me remark, how honourably Mr. Campbell behaved to Charles and the gentlemen who lodged under his roof. No money, no bribe could make him violate the ſacred laws of hoſpitality, and fix an eternal ſtain on his family. Even though it was well known that this gentleman was ſtrictly loyal and well attached to the reigning Family, yet the enormous ſum of thirty thouſand pounds could not bribe him to act the infamous part required. The maſter of a noted family, a very bulky man, who is now alive, and reſides in an iſland in that country, with the clergyman at their head, landed before day, with a boat full of armed men, on the Iſle of Glaſs, with a determined reſolution to ſeize the Chevalier, and ſecure the bribe offered by Government.

Mr.

Mr. Campbell scorned the bribe, and expostulated much against the infamous attempt; he also pointed out the danger of making the experiment on so many formidable and desperate gentlemen who would chop the heads off the whole of them before they sheathed their swords. But when he found that they still persisted in spite of reason, he assured them, that he himself would fall in his cause, rather than give up the man that intrusted him with his life, or entail shame on his posterity. With that view he dispatched his son to give them intelligence of their danger. The Chevalier and his party were forewarned, and armed before that gentleman arrived, and were ready to give the assailants a hot reception, had they approached; but they sneaked off from the island, ashamed, and disappointed at the loss of the money, which they already had devoured in their thoughts, and divided to every man in his due proportion.

But, to return from this noble-minded gentleman to our little tyranical country Surgeon.

Soon after he had acquired poffeffion of the vaft tract of country already mentioned, he began, with undaunted courage, to double the rents of the fubtenants, either by adding more money to their former rents, or by adding two or more tenants to one bay or town, by taking iflands from another, by extorting fome tuns of fea-ware for kelp from a third, though their land fhould want manure and themfelves bread; nay, and to erect new bays in places formerly altogether uninhabited. Inftead of fix days he added fifty-two days yearly, to be paid, along with all the fervices and cafualties laid on, as already mentioned, by the preceding tackfman. Being determined that he fhould not fail through delicacy like his predeceffors, while the people were mafters of a fhilling he will have it, or they muft remove; and as they had no other place to go to, he was fure that he would make them yield to his terms.

At fo unufual and terrible an attack on the poor people, they cried out moft loudly, and were much furprifed that the land fteward

ard did not interfere with his authority: but as he was the man that gave them over to be hired out for this man's advantage, it was in vain to apply to him; yet their cafe was truly diftreffing, for the fea-ware which they had for the cold mofs, being the only ftimulus to make it bear, was not only taken from them, but alfo the time for making the ground ready for it, was taken likewife.

It may not be improper to mention here, as a circumftance defcriptive of the Weftern Hebrides, that before he dared to practife thofe oppreffions, he thought it advifeable to fortify himfelf by a ftrong matrimonial alliance. This he did by marrying an old maiden lady; who, in her younger days, would have treated the idea of being united to fuch a man, with the utmoft fcorn. Although old refidenters claim a kind of prefcriptive right of oppreffion, they do not allow the fame right to new in-comers, whom they confider as interlopers, unlefs they initiate and ingraft themfelves, as it were, among the old tackfmen, if not among the lairds, by marriage.

Before I quit this extraordinary character, I muft yet relate the following anecdote.

He was patronized, when a very young practitioner in phyfic and furgery, by old Clanronald, whom he fleeced of a large fum of money, in the following manner. He was engaged by that good-natured chief, or rather contrived to be engaged by him, to adminifter medicines occafionally among his poor tenantry in South Uift. This eafy gentleman, to encourage fo laborious a phyfician, bound and obliged himfelf by a bond, already prepared by the fkilful practitioner, to be forthcoming for any deficiency in point of payment on the part of his tenants.--- With this fecurity in his pocket, fubfcribed by Clanronald, he was encouraged to exercife his unlimited commiffion with indefatigable induftry, over this extenfive diftrict; and marked with great care his charge againft them, accurately dated, for his faithful attendance.

The old gentleman being in his dotage, and perhaps in his cups, when he fubfcribed the bond, forgot to mention the deed to his

his active lady, who was ignorant of the matter until some time thereafter. When her husband was dead and buried, the account was presented to her for payment, and a demand made.

The lady, astonished and enraged at so glaring an advantage taken of her unsuspicious husband, denied the justice of the charge, and desired the infamous bond to be thrown into the fire.

But here, for the first time, her ladyship found her mistake in this man; for in him she found no longer the fawning, flattering cringer, who carefully attended on her husband's bowl, but the forward, daring, impudent fellow, as her ladyship said in her passion.

He assured her ladyship, that the money he was determined to have; and accordingly sued for it at law. She defended her cause before the court at Edinburgh, and represented the dangerous man in a proper point of view; and his artfully practising on her husband's weak fide, to pick his pockets. The force of thefe arguments the whole Court faw, but as he was in poffeffion of the bond, though infamoufly obtained, the law was fo clear on his fide, that fentence was given in his favour, and thus he triumphed over the defrauded lady.

After this conteft with the lady of the manor, he had penetration enough to underftand that her country was likely to be too hot for him to refide in; and as the gentlemen and people had taken the alarm againft the man whofe intrigues they formerly only fufpected, he judged it advifeable to pack up his chefts of medicine, feeing all his hopes of drawing more into a fimilar fnare were quite blafted.

He now began to look about where he fhould next lay down his boxes. In Lewis they were too well acquainted with him; for the low countries he had not fufficient knowledge; and his own country he abhors, becaufe he wifely recollected, that a prophet had no honour there. In thefe circumftances,

ces, he turned his face to the wild hills of Harris, and took a ten year's leafe of Lufkintire.

And now, to give to all thefe particulars concerning this oppreffive and fraudulent man, fome connection with a general defcription of the ftate of fociety. Through his great influence and power he has obtained a kind of clerical dignity; having been created a SENATOR, or ELDER of the Church: of which order of men in general, but particularly the Elders of Harris, as well as the ftate of religion in the Weftern Hebrides, I fhall have occafion to fpeak afterwards: from a review of all which it will manifeftly appear, that religious, not lefs then civil matters, in the Weftern Hebrides, are much influenced by their remote diftance from the feat of Government.

The tackfman next to be mentioned is the Rev. Mr. Macleod, minifter of Harris: a man, who, from the loweft origin, has, by talents, infinuation, and addrefs, attained to great wealth, influence, and authority.

This

This gentleman has a kind of legiflative authority for making country regulations. His ordinances, the tenants maintain, are framed to fupport the rich and diftrefs the poor. As thefe, however, have no vote in the courts of juftice, their bufinefs is to bear the yoke and keep filent.

As the baron bailie feldom holds any courts, every tackfman is invefted with the full powers of the barons, only they dare not intermeddle with the four pleas of the crown. I could never learn that they ventured to hang any man at thefe private courts; but for other petty crimes they horfe-whip them, and even fcourge them tied up naked to a poft. It will eafily be credited, that fcourging their fervants is common, when we find it practifed even by their minifters of religion: of an inftance of which I myfelf was witnefs.

A ftout fellow, named M'Corcle, fon to the hen-wife (caillach nan ceark) that lived near, was detected one evening in taking a mouthful of barley meal out of an old cheft, through a hole made by
the

the mice; very deftructive creatures, and particularly to this youth, being the means of leading him into a trap that made him groan. The fellow having nothing to plead but hunger, was found guilty, and fentence was pronounced for whipping on a ftated day, with his hands tied, and his body bound to a ftake.

All the tenants were fummoned to attend at the execution of this fentence, and ordered each to bring his family, that they might learn therefrom what each of themfelves had to expect in cafe any of them were ever detected at fuch criminal practices in time coming.

But as there is no hangman in all this extenfive eftate, no one of the tenants would become driver; therefore the reverend perfonage took on himfelf an office fo confiftent with the religion which he profeffed to teach! And accordingly, he and his lady led forth the criminal, ftripped him of his rags, bound him to the ftake, and began a very heavy exercife upon the bare buff of the delinquent, when he received many a fevere ftripe. But the cries of caillach nan ceark,

ceark, his mother, the clappings of hands, tearing of her hair, beating of her breaſt, and running herſelf out of breath, till at length ſhe fainted away, made every ſoul preſent ſad and ſorrowful.

The Sabbath following, he was led to the church, with a bag of meal about his neck, a humiliating ſpectacle to the pariſhioners, who were given to know thereby what each of themſelves, ſhould he tranſgreſs, had to expect from the hands of the reverend executioner. At this new ſpectacle the people are ſaid to have emitted a confuſed noiſe, and turned away their eyes with (a bhuain, a bhuain! Cha bè ſhud ar miniſtar beannuight Aulay, ach nfior bhruit fon cleochd) " Away with it! This, ſaid they, was not the leſſon taught by their bleſſed miniſter, old Aulay, but that of a beaſt under the appearance of a parſon to inſult them."

This oppreſſor exacts the ſame rigorous terms of work and days, with all other caſualties, from his ſubtenants and ſcallags, that the two laſt-mentioned ones demand. And the people are no leſs loud in their complaints

plaints againſt the poverty of their diets. Many of them prefer their own, though at his work; no ſmall mortification to a ſpirit ſo inflated with pride and haughtineſs. But being in the heart of his wife's connections, many of his overbearing oppreſſions muſt be borne with, for fear of offending them; for no clergyman could be ſafe if he attempted any thing that would border on oppreſſion, being either unconnected by matrimony, or affinity, with ſuch as did belong to the country; and of courſe, leſs intitled to the favour of the gentlemen of the place.

And moſt of the cautious, artful gentlemen, whoſe fine leaſes are almoſt expired, caſt their caps at his feet, leſt his buſy intermeddling diſpoſition ſhould lead him to open the eyes of the managers to ſet them on ſearching out the real profits that are paid by the lower ſubtenants, and ruin that branch of their profitable gain, as well as the great benefits that ſome of them reap from the ſub-miſſive conduct of their tenantry, who are afraid of offending their old maſters, leſt they ſhould fall under the mercy of the

late

late incumbents, whofe conduct is terror compleat.—

Strange as it may appear, it is a fact, that if an innocent gentleman fhould unfortunately fall under the lafh of thefe tyrants, inftead of a reparation for the abufe, which they are confcious of having committed, their rage increafes, wantonly, and without caufe: fo far are they from making an apology, or giving redrefs, that the injured man incurs their hatred more and more, and their rage is converted gradually into down-right malice. So true is the obfervation of Tacitus, *proprium humani ngenii eft odiffe quem læferis.* " It is natural to the human heart to hate the man whom you have injured."

## CHAP. IV.

*Of the Genius, Customs, Manners, and Dress of the Western Hebrideans.*

HAVING said so much concerning proprietors, tacksmen, subtenants, and scallags, we shall now turn our attention to their genius, customs, manners, dress, and modes of life.

The Western Hebrideans are, in general, naturally possessed of strong parts, quick and penetrating in their apprehensions, perhaps in a much higher degree than is to be met with in the heart of any inland country. This must arise from their frequent intercourse with different characters of men, to which their connection with navigation daily exposes them, and forces them to be cautious, active, and insinuating. Besides this, their constant danger from that
element,

element, with which they are fo converfant, renders it abfolutely neceffary to have their eyes and wit perpetually exercifed for their prefervation; and that cuftom becomes a confirmed habit that difplays itfelf in all their ordinary commerce through life.

They have a fine vein for poetry and mufic, both vocal and inftrumental: more efpecially in both the Uifts; where one may meet, not only with ftudied, but even extemporaneoeus effufions of the moft acute and pointed fatire, that pierce to the heart, and leave a poignant fting.

At the fame time, in thefe compofitions one meets with the moft foft and tender ftrains of feeling affection, that melt the foul with heart - felt fenfibility and love, along with the moft moving dirges and lamentations for their loft fweet-hearts and friends; and the whole compofed by the vulgar, no lefs than by the moft refined. In thefe qualities they excel any of the Englifh or old Scots fongs, which have hitherto been publifhed, however much and defervedly celebrated and admired by every true

true judge of mufical compofitions. And had the language been fo generally underftood, the Gâlic mufic would have been introduced, with admiration and delight, on every ftage on which tafte and elegance prevailed.

Their *luinneags*, with the chorus of the band, are inconceiveably agreeable to the ear; and the manner of turning the hands and hankerchiefs, when united in the circle, is no lefs entertaining to the eye. Vocal and inftrumental mufic make up part of their entertainments. In their agility in the dance, they ftand almoft unrivalled by any people. In Lewis, fince their late happy change from fervitude to freedom by the prefent nobleminded proprietor, they are, animated with fuch life as to meet in companies, regularly every week, at ftated places, where both old and young take their turn at this agreeable paftime; when they exercife themfelves with amazing alertnefs and fpirit. Their muficians receive regular falaries. The violin is more ufed on thefe occafions than the fmall pipes. This laft, with the great pipe, is moftly ufed in the field, at weddings, funerals, and other public meetings. The piper muft play

play up a *Cuart Phibrachd*, a march that is heard at a great diftance, and produces a fine effect on the fpirits of the company. Moft of the great families had their pipers to play before the doors, or in the great hall, during meal-time, and appointed certain lands for their fupport, which continued in the families time immemorial. Some ftill retain this ancient cuftom. The M'Cruimmans of Sky hold their lands from Macleod of Macleod, ftill as their family feat, for attending the chief's perfon and family.

There is no diftinct account, at what time this farm was granted to them. Thefe famous people had a kind of college for teaching young men that branch of mufic, and qualifying them to make a fuperior appearance in public, to fuch as have only common advantages.

The principal piper of another great chief from the Ifles is now profeffor of that branch of mufic in Edinburgh, and is attended by feveral fcholars; and fome of them frequently gain the premiums given by the HIGHLAND SOCIETY of London, to be annually competed

peted for in that metropolis. Of the merit of the candidates the profeſſor, and other competent gentlemen, are the judges.

The common people are wonderfully ingenious; even the women as well as the men are weavers. They learn that trade in a few months. But they are often interrupted by the tackſmen, who pretend that they are ſpoiling the cloth; but in reality want to oblige theſe manufacturers to betake themſelves to their ſervice, for they do not care though they ſhould wear ſkins inſtead of cloth, provided they can promote their own ends by ſecuring the labours of theſe weavers. Theſe objections are the more attended to, when under the ſanction of their country regulations they are ſupported by authority. It is very common to find men who are taylors, ſhoe-makers, ſtocking-weavers, coopers, carpenters, and ſawyers of timber; ſome of them employ the plane, the ſaw, the adze, the wimble, and they even groove the deals, for cheſts. They make hooks for fiſhing, caſt metal buckles, broaches, and rings for their favourite females. They make nets of different kinds for fiſhing, with all the other tackle

tackle and neceffary implements: fome of them even make, as well as mend, their own boats. As for the other implements, as ploughs, harrows, rakes, *cafs chrom*, and *cafs direach*, neceffary for hufbandry, every man is more or lefs ufed to make them. The women wake the cloth on an implement of ten feet long, and three feet broad, made of wicker, called *cleadh luaidh*, and fometimes the frame is made of thick deals, indented or hollowed, to make it rough for the webs. Four or five women fit on each fide of this frame, working the cloth to and fro, either by their hands or feet, with a little ftraw below themfelves and this frame, to keep them from the ground. On thefe occafions, the *iorrams* and *luinneags* begin with great fpirit; one of them fings the ftanza, while all the reft unite in the chorus, which they repeat twice or thrice after each ftanza. The fweet melody of their mufic feldom fails to collect a number of hearers, who join in the fong.

The men wear the fhort coat, the feila-beg, and the fhort hofe, with bonnets fewed with black ribbons around their rims, and
a flit

a flit behind with the fame ribbon in a knot. Their coats are commonly tartan, ftriped with black, red, or fome other colour, after a pattern made, upon a ftick, of the yarn, by themfelves, or fome other ingenious contriver. Their waiftcoats are either of the fame, or fome fuch ftuff; but the feilabegs are commonly of breacan, or fine Stirling plaids, if their money can afford them.

At common work they ufe either fhort or long coats and breeches made of ftriped cloth, and many of them very coarfe, according to their work. Their fhirts are commonly made of wool; and however coarfe they may appear to ftrangers, they are allowed to conduce much to the health and longevity for which this country is famous; as I have known them eighty, ninety, and fome even a hundred years old, in thefe iflands, and able to do their daily work.

When they go in queft of the herring, they drefs fomething like the failors, but of coarfer cloth, with hats over their eyes, to mark the fifh the better. They are careful about

about drying their nets, and other fiſhing tackle.

Their brogues (ſhoes) are made of cow or horſe leather, and often of ſeals ſkins, that are commonly well tanned by the root of tormintile, which they dig out from the hillocks, and uncultivated lands, about the ſea-ſide. This, properly pounded and prepared, without either lime or bark, is ſufficient to make the hides pliant and fit for wearing. It anſwers their purpoſe much better than leather tanned with lime or bark, becauſe they ſeldom grow hard or ſhrink when dried, even though wet all day; which is not the caſe with ſuch as are burnt with lime. They never uſe tan-pits, but bind the hides faſt with ropes, and hold them for ſeveral days in ſome remote ſolitary ſtream, until the hair begins to come off, of its own accord; and after that, the tormintile roots are applied for bark, as above deſcribed. Such of the men as can afford them, wear large foreſt coats above their other garb, eſpecially on Sundays, or at the public meetings, as weddings, burials, or fairs. Either in this or a coarſe coarfe breacan *(i. e.* the plaid) with their beft apparel, they appear on thefe folemn occafions; but many of thofe who are poor, and cannot afford it, often do and muft appear in their tattered clothes and dirty fhirts, without either ftockings or brogues, quite barefooted, even in froft and fnow, in diftrefs fufficient to extort compaffion from every perfon, but fuch tyrants as are the caufe of fo much mifery to thofe ftarved creatures, who are often creeping along with white or ftriped petticoats belonging to their wives, or daughters and fifters, about their fhoulders.

The women wear long or fhort gowns, with a waiftcoat and two petticoats, moftly of the ftripes or tartan, as already defcribed, except the lower coat, which is white. The married wives wear linen mutches, or caps, either faftened with ribbons of various colours, or with tape ftraps, if they cannot afford ribbons. All of them wear a fmall plaid, a yard broad, called *guilechan,* about their fhoulders, faftened by a large broach. The broaches are generally round, and of filver, if the wearer be in tolerable circumftances: if poor, the broaches, being either circular

cular or triangular, are of bafer metal and modern date. The firft kind has been worn time immemorial even by the ladies. The *arrifats* are quite laid afide in all this country, by the different ranks of women; being the moft ancient drefs ufed by that clafs. It confifted of one large piece of flannel, that reached down to the fhoe, and faftened with clafps below, and the large filver broach at the breaft, while the whole arm was entirely naked. The ladies made ufe of the finer, while common women ufed coarfer kinds of flannel, or white woollen cloths. The married women bind up their hair with a large pin into a knot on the crown of their heads, below their linens; and the unmarried frequently go bare-headed, with their hair bound up with ribbons, or garters. They often wear linen caps, called mutches, particularly on Sabbaths. Many of the more wealthy appear at church with a profufion of ribbons and head-dreffes, with cloaks, and high-heeled fhoes. Thofe whofe circumftances cannot admit of that, muft appear with one of their petticoats, either tartan, or of one colour, around their fhoulders, on Sundays, as well as on week days. They feldom

dom travel any where without this appendage; nay, in the houfe, when at fuch work as will admit of it; feeing it would be thought naked in a woman to go without it: it alfo defends them from the inclemency of the weather. Moft of them wear napkins, or handkerchiefs, on their necks; and many of the richeft of them ufe filk ones, whether black or fpotted, as fuits their fancies.

Frequently the old women wear little *guilechans*, (fmall plaids) about their fhoulders, and woollen hoods about their heads, with very coarfe linen under them faftened with a pin below their chins. The *breeid*, or curtah, a fine linen handkerchief faftened about married women's heads, with a flap hanging behind their backs, above the guilechan, is moftly laid afide.

Moft of the poorer tenants cannot afford to wear brogues in Summer, unlefs they are obliged to be treading among the fharp rocks on the fhores, at their mafter's kelp, when the mafter muft fupply them, except they can afford to provide for themfelves. It would be too great a luxury for a poor one

to

to ufe them, unlefs at the fame, or fimilar rugged employment. Nothing fhort of extreme neceffity obliges them to appear in public meetings in thefe humiliating garbs; for otherwife their pride would revolt at the very thought of fuch fhabby dreffes.

They converfe familiarly with one another by the term of *naby*, or neighbour; or *carrid*, a friend; *ghaole*, or *cagger*, love; and fuch endearing expreffions; but, though naturally frank, they are very referved to ftrangers at firft: yet they modeftly afk a vaft many queftions from every ftranger whom they chance to meet; that being the only vehicle through which they can hear of public tranfactions carried on in the country or nation at large.

On that account, any man that wifhes to pafs the nights at any of their huts, muft be at pains to collect all the news, by making regular enquiries, as he paffes along, and when they are carefully arranged, and properly delivered, he is fure of meeting with a hearty reception. His hiftory is believed

like

like oracles, which they faithfully retail to their neighbours; and are sure of reciprocal returns on similar occasions, displaying the same inquisitive spirit and hospitality with the Germans, as described by Tacitus.

The huts of the oppressed tenants are remarkably naked and open; quite destitute of furniture, except logs of timbers collected from the wrecks of the sea, to sit on about the fire, which is placed in the middle of the house, or upon seats made of straw, like foot hassacks, stuffed with straw or stubble. Many of them must rest satisfied with large stones placed around the fire, in order. As all persons must have their own blankets to sleep in, they make their beds in whatever corner suits their fancy, and in the mornings they fold them up into a small compass, with all their gowns, cloaks, coats, and petticoats, that are not in use.

The cows, goats, and sheep, with the ducks, hens, and dogs, must have the common benefit of the fire, and particularly the

young

young and tendereft are admitted next to it.

This filthy fty is never cleaned but once a-year, when they place the dung on the fields as manure for barley crops. Thus from the neceffity of laying litter below thefe cattle to keep them dry, the dung naturally increafes in height almoft mid-wall high, fo that the men fit low about the fire, while the cattle look down from above upon the company.

It is true they are at pains to keep the fty as dry as poffible, by attending on the their cows with large veffels to throw out the wafh; but ftill it muft be wet and unwholfome, and no argument can prevail on them to turn out the dung on a dunghill daily, as they have got the idea impreffed on their minds, that the air carries off the ftrength if much expofed. Indeed many of them make little or no ufe of the unmixed dung that is piled up by heaps about their doors; but fince the mafters have taken much of the kelp, which was their ufual manure, from the poor creatures, to burn it

for

for the markets, they are forced to make better ufe of the dung. In the heart of Lewis, where many of the farms are far from the fea, they are neceffitated not only to ufe all manner of cow dung, but even to ftrip the houfe of its thatch every Spring, to make an addition to their manure for the lands.

But thofe farmers who are bleffed with the protection of their lairds, live much more comfortably, as they can feparate the houfed cattle from their fire-fides, by little partitions, but fo open as to allow the benefit of the fire to reach their cattle, though ftill the whole of them, whether rich or poor, keep the cow-houfes without cleaning them till Spring.

Every fubtenant muft have his own beams and other fide timbers. Four or five couples, with their complement of fide timbers, are reckoned a good fufficiency for a hut. The walls of them are fix feet thick, packed with mofs or earth in the middle, with a facing of rough ftones built on both fides. This is called a ftall, and commonly belongs to the

the mafter: upon this the timbers are erected, as follow:

First, the beams and spars are bound together by ropes made of heather or bent, and placed standing on these stalls. Then the side rafters are fastened with ropes to those beams pretty fast, and the rows of ropes wrought very close, so as to keep the stubble with which the houses are thatched from falling through. For the beams and roof tree, with the side timbers, could not bear the weight of *divats* above them, and therefore the ropes must be the thicker plaited over them.

Having laid the stubble over the side timbers, interwoven with ropes, they secure this thatch with heather ropes thrown across the roof of the huts, and these are fastened below with large stones which are fixed to their ends, and hang dangling over the sides of the walls to keep all fast, that the winds and storms, which are frequent here, may not strip the huts of their covers.

The moment that a poor man is obliged to remove, he immediately unties the timbers of his hut, and bundles up the rotten thatch, which he wafts in his little Norway fmack to the place appointed.

It is then obvious, from the nature of their huts, and the uncertainty of their refidence in one place, that their accommodations muft be very uncomfortable; I mean only the oppreffed ones; that their huts muft be unfpeakably naked, without furniture, except a loom, or old cheft to hold their eatables, and a few plates or facks made of benty grafs. They make a number of bags of fheep-fkins for holding their meal, with a few other fuch articles as fortune and their own ingenuity procure.

Their doors, if they have any fhutters, ftand moftly open, as they feldom lock them at nights; and their windows are but holes made through the thatch, immediately above the fide walls. Thefe, with the chimney top, ftand open to admit day-light. Thefe huts, being thus without locks to their doors, and without feparate apartments, we need not be
furprifed

surprised to find the virtue of their women too often severely tried; and no wonder though the poor unprotected females suffer in such circumstances; and they must be miserably exposed in gentlemen's kitchens, where the men and women sleep without any head to keep a kind of awe over them, for all their kitchens are separated from the main dwelling apartments of the family.

Every beggar, male and female, must carry their blankets on their backs in a kind of sack made of grass, from house to house, to sleep in; and they require to carry no other burthen of meal or other eatables, but they are fed from the same dish with the people in whose house they lodge.

We may observe that this must bear very hard on the poor men and women-servants, who are forced by country statutes to serve almost for nothing, except their scanty bit of bread, and obliged to work at the severe exercises of carrying the panniers full either of sea-ware or horse dung upon their backs; and yet be under the necessity of providing bed and body clothes of their own; even

worse

worfe off than the beafts of burden, who are commonly furnifhed with harnefs, fitted for the yoke or load, by their mafters.

The wages of a full-grown active maid amounts to five fhillings fterling a year, and leffened or increafed in proportion to her age, or fuppofed merit; and out of thefe few fhillings, fhe muft repay any damage of tea-cups, or other articles that may fuffer through her hands.

The yearly wages of the men fervants bear the fame proportion with the women's; for there are no day-labourers for daily wages here as in other countries---no fuch thing is ever allowed or encouraged by the oppreffors; but fuch people muft become fcallags, and yield their labour for lefs profits than even the young fervant men do; for the labourer, or fcallag, muft hang about his helplefs wife and family, whereas the fervant man often betakes himfelf to the fea fervice, to get out of their reach.

The wages of their men are various. According to the ftated country ftatutes, the man who has the management of the farm, and working people to direct, may have from two to three pounds, if very deserving, and the honour of eating his meat by himself, by way of respect. He is honoured by the name of Grey-fear, or Bailiff.

The lower servants may be hired from forty to thirty, and even from twenty to ten shillings per annum. I myself engaged an active lad for my servant for twenty shillings, and he thought himself wonderfully fortunate. He had compleated his twentieth year, when he entered my service, and the year preceding he received only ten shillings sterling from his former master, who obliged him to serve most of the former time for less. With his twenty shillings, and the difference of his employment, he dressed like a gentleman in comparison with others of his years; and that lad would think himself rich indeed, with thirty or forty shillings for the following years. But all these common men servants are obliged to make up any damage, either by the breaking in of horses or cattle on green standing corn under night, or the loss of cattle, if under their charge; and
many

many of them also have been obliged, at the expiration of their terms, to leave their oppressors in their debt, until their time of re-entering the service returned again by rotation.

Those servants also receive brogues, to enable them to bear the panniers of sea-weed from the shores, and I leave it to my reader to reflect with himself, whether the man or woman have worn the value of the wages, supposing the highest even forty shillings to the man and five shillings to the woman, though no deductions were made for the little damage sustained through accidents; so that one might fairly conclude that, with bed and body clothes, both these classes of servants are not gainers by their service. But they are only used as beasts of burden, and the masters reap the advantage.

It is but just to observe, that this extreme severity is not used any where over this whole country, except where the country regulations force them into practice; but the profits arising from this lately introduced mode of severity, are so tempting, that it is gaining rather than losing ground even

by

by thofe who are inclined to be more humane. Not very many of the old honourable refidenters force their tenants to remove yearly, from place to place, with their poor families. This mild treatment enables them to make feparate apartments for their bed and board, with their little furniture; by which means they feparate the fexes; and the women, if they are willing, may protect their virtue from injuries; and their looks and drefs befpeak them a different people. As for the poor tenants, who are under the laird's protection, they begin to feel the bleffing of emancipation from the yoke of the tackfmen, and look back with compaffion on thofe who ftill remain under thefe fevere mafters.

In defiance of the hardfhips thefe oppreffed people fuffer, they retain part of their former ftate and dignity, at their meetings and partings. They addrefs one another by the title of gentleman or lady, (duinuasle and bheanuasle) and embrace one another moft cordially, with bonnets off. And they are never known to enter a door
without

without blessing the house and people so loud as to be heard, and embracing every man and woman belonging to the family. They both give and receive news, and are commonly entertained with the best fare their entertainers are able to afford.

The beggars are much respected among the commonality. The hosts know that these were once equal, if not superior to themselves in point of wealth; for it unfortunately happens in many parts of this country, when a man becomes so frail as not to be in a capacity to look after his flock of sheep in person, that he is very rapidly stript of them, and that frequently by his near relations. However astonishing it may appear to strangers, it is a known fact, that those nimble fellows can catch the wildest sheep that feeds on the highest hills by swiftness of foot, and that in the night as well as by day. I have seen boys of twelve years of age, who were so trained to this office, that they would not only run them down, but for diversion suffer them to escape, that they might have the pleasure of a second race, to take them again ; and that

through

through the moſt rugged rocks and precipices. The ſheep, over moſt of this country, are extremely wild, ſeeing moſt of them muſt be caught by dogs trained for that uſe; a circumſtance which makes them fly at the ſight of man or dog; but the thieves dare not uſe dogs, for fear of being ſeen, or heard by their noiſe, and they are bred to catch ſheep in their younger days, by their parents, without the uſe and help of dogs, in broad day, to exerciſe them.

By the laws of the country no poor man dares make uſe of a ſheep's head for four or five days after ſhe is killed, that every one who pleaſes may examine the ear-mark. I have ſeen a ſheep's head taken from a man by the real owner, and kept for ten years, to prove the theft againſt him before the court.

Thus the effects of an old man will ſoon be devoured by his neighbours. He gradually becomes unfit to do his work, or pay his rents, and of courſe he muſt diſmantle his houſe, diſpoſe of his roof, while he muſt take up his bed and walk about with this burden.

In the back settlements of Harris, neither the love of God, nor fear of man, could prevail with a master to allow the scallag the liberty of living under his own roof, to shelter his aged body from the inclemency of the seasons, without taking a little piece of moss, for labour and rent, from the oppressors, who make the best of the lands; nor are huts allowed in Harris, without lands, and for their service. But a friendly disposition towards the poor is manifested by the gentlemen towards the poor gentlemen and ladies of their order, that sink through misfortunes or extravagance. These are admitted to their better tables, and used with easy familiarity.

They burn the straw of the sheaf, to make the oats dry for meal: and though the grain is black by the ashes, and the meal coloured, yet it is not unpleasant to the taste, and it is thought to be very wholesome food. This, with most of their oatmeal, they grind on *braabs*, a kind of mill similar to the quern, but made of harder stone, and of the same magnitude with quern millstones, being about three feet in diameter, and four or five

five inches thick. The uppermost stone is turned round by the hand of one or two women, who grind as much meal, evening and morning, as serves for the day.

They have also some of the old Highland mills, that are driven about by water. Those mills are rude, and extremely simple in their constructions, being only one wheel that drives round the spindle, which is fastened to the upper grinding millstone. These mills are slow, and at such distances from the huts of the tenants, that in general they prefer their *braahs* or querns.

Their cakes are made of barley meal, and toasted against a stone placed upright before a good fire; and sometimes, when either haste or hunger impels them, they are laid on the ashes, with more ashes above, to bake them more quickly. The people eat twice a day. The first meal is called *deinnar* or breakfast, the last is their supper. They seldom break fast, unless from some necessary haste, before eleven o'clock; and the supper, when night drives them home from their labour, is placed before them.

Potatoes

Potatoes and fish generally make up their first meal, and the whole family commonly eat out of one dish called the *claar*. This large dish is between three and four feet in length, and a foot and a half in breadth, made up of deal. They place the straw or grass on the bottom, and pour out the potatoes and fish above that stratum, which they generally collect carefully, with the fragments, for some favourite cow. Their last meal is generally made up of *brochan*, (a kind of water gruel) boiled mutton, with bread and potatoes, at their own houses, if in any tolerable circumstances, and under mild masters: but no such luxuries are to be met in any other kitchens, nor can it be expected in the families of the oppressed. These must search for cuddies, or such fish as are on the coasts, such as cod, dog-fish, faiths, skait, &c.

In time of eating these poor meals, their doors are generally shut, and few people chuse to enter when they find them shut. It is difficult to account for this general custom among a people so universally hospitable. They can assign no reason for this churlish piece

piece of conduct but custom. I suppose it took its origin from the times that that country, as well all Scotland, was infested by a set of robbers called *Cearnachs*, who went about in bands fully armed, and would force their way into any house where they supposed any meat could be found, and generally took it by force. Probably the impression of those practices remained on the minds of succeeding generations; and that practice originating in necessity, obtained the force of a custom, and continued long after that necessity ceased.

Indeed all the Scots, even to the fourteenth century, were strangers to the luxuries of life. When Randolf, Earl of Murray, and Sir James Douglas, in the reign of Robert Bruce, invaded the north of England, and after Douglas had performed extraordinary feats of prowess, the Scots returned home, and left some hundred bags made of deer skins, all full of water and flesh for the use of the men; and a thousand wooden spits, with meat on them, which was roasted. They were so contrived as to answer for kettles. "And," Macpherson observes, in his Dissertation,

tation, " that this one specimen of simple cookery is still used among the Highlanders in hunting parties." Nay, I spoke with a man who saw the thief boiling a bag full of meat with a gentle fire held below, while he constantly rubbed the bottom with grease, fastened to a stick, to keep it from burning."

Both men and women are fond of tobacco; the men commonly chew it, and beg a little from every gentleman; and there is no travelling through those countries without a certain quantity of that article in company. The gentlemen fill their nostrils with long quids of it, and these, when thrown away, are gathered carefully by the poorer sort, for a second turn. Instances can be produced, where a servant has consumed his whole yearly wages on this single article of luxury.

In passing to and from the islands, tobacco is necessary to a gentleman, if he wishes to avoid both delay and imposition. Here it deserves to be remarked, that though the gentlemen do squeeze subtenants themselves, yet they do not discourage, nay, some of the

the bafer kind of mafters encourage the poor oppreffed creatures to make heavy charges on ftrangers; and I could produce inftances when complaints were juftly lodged againft impofition. To prevent thofe grofs charges, any knowing man will deal his tobacco liberally, and in that event, he is fure of a fpeedy and very cheap paflage, *or convoy*, through the different ifles.

The men keep their tobacco in leather bags made of feal fkins, called *fpleuchans*, which keep the tobacco foft and taftely.

The old women make ufe of their tobacco in fnuff made into graddan, the fame with the Irifh blackguard, which they generally keep in fea nuts that grow on the large tangles or red fea-ware, and which are fometimes found upon the fhores. This nut is about feven inches in circumference, and one half inch thick, full of kernel, which is carefully digged out through a fmall round hole made on purpofe. Out of this hole the fnuff is fhaken on the palms of their hands, and taken out with a pen made for the purpofe. Thefe fhells, or nuts, are very precious,

cious, and by the richer people are bound in silver. There are several other kinds of sea nuts, of different makes, that are held in high veneration among the vulgar for their supposed efficacy on several occasions, and they are particularly used about children.

The common, as well as better sort of people, court sweet-hearts at nights, over all this country. The unlocked doors yield those lovers but too easy access to their favourites. The natural consequences of their rencounters often occasion squabbles in kirk courts, in which the minister and elders take cognizance of the fornication committed in the parish.

This inquisitorial office is generally more agreeable to the elders, than to the ministers; as they are the more ignorant and insignificant, and consequently require more the prop of other people's failings. In cases, however, in which the ministers are governed either by a druidical rigour of temper, or by hypocrisy, they too exercise great severity against the incontinent, in various parts of Scotland; as

the

the reader will find in the ingenious Captain Newte's Tour. This severity, however, is not often productive of the amendment pretended to be designed. I say *pretended*, for in many instances they, who are at least shrewdly suspected of lewdness, as well as intemperance themselves, are the severest and most curious and prying inquisitors into the failings of others.

In the part of the country we are describing, however, this frailty still prevails with the favourite fair, and her intercourse is frequently with so many men, that the unfortunate girl is often at a nonplus where to fix with certainty; but she seldom fails to give up the gentleman or single man, to save the married man and herself from the shame of doing penance in a white sheet. The rich man, indeed, finds a substitute, by giving a little bribe, and a great many fine promises, both to the woman and the ostensible father. As the poor young men cannot pay for substitutes, the contending parties must submit the issue of their cause to an oath; and the affidavit of the suspected satisfies the accuser, and the

bastard

baftard is as much efteemed as the lawfully begotten child.

The woman, if fhe is pregnant by a gentleman, is by no means looked down upon, but is provided in a hufband with greater eclat than without forming fuch a connection. Inftead of being defpifed, numberlefs inftances can be produced, where pregnant women have been difputed for, and even fought for, by the different fuitors.

Their daily implements of fifhing are the rod, and the *taubh*, or net. This laft is a pock-net, bound round a large circular ring of wands or hoops, and that tied to the end of a long pole of eight feet in length. By throwing a little boiled wilks, chewed out of their mouths, over the top of it, when funk below the furface, the cuddies will get in after the meat, and when they are on the bottom, the upper part is elevated above the fea, and fome hundreds are catched, at times, at each dipping.

Inftead of iron crooks they ufe a ftick of four feet long, full of holes, with a pin to

pafs

pafs through to raife or lower their pots when placed above their fires. The pots are fufpended from the roof, in the middle of the houfe, by a rope made of benty grafs. They make a kind of coarfe crockery ware, for boiling water and dreffing victuals.

They make very neat wooden locks, * both for their doors and chefts. They are made of the fame materials: and I have feen pieces of wooden workmanfhip, fuch as trunks, chefts, and tobacco-pipes, fo well made, and elegantly engraved, as would not difgrace the moft capital artifts.

Gâlic is the common language over all this country: but their intercourfe with fifhers and paffengers to and from other countries, introduce a mixture of words from the Englifh and other nations. This mixture will gradually fpoil that nervous expreffive tongue.

The

---

* It may be worthy of remark here, that notwithftanding the various improvements in lock-making for centuries paft, none that I have heard of has been proof againft the pick-lock, except that invented by BRAMAH, of Piccadilly, London, which is conftructed upon the principle of this rude implement.

The poor are totally deftitute of letters. All the laudable and charitable contributions fent for inftructing them in the knowledge of the Scriptures, have been wantonly perverted by artful, defigning politicians; as will appear when we fpeak of the religious inftitutions eftablifhed by law.

The men are extremely fond of fpirituous liquors, when they can fall in with them. When they can meet with a cafk, they feldom part with it, till it is emptied. The quarrels arifing from drunkennefs are more general than the combats of Englifhmen;— and more hurtful, as the victors do not fpare the proftrate enemy.

In Lewis, the iflands of Harris and the Uifts, they make whifkey of oats, but not of barley. They have alfo abundance of rum, brandy, gin, and wines, which are fmuggled into the country: but the charges made in retailing of thefe fpirits become fo extravagant, that the poor people cannot eafily touch any. On certain folemn occafions, however, they have recourfe to thofe foreign fpirits. Had Mr. Pennant, at thofe times,

times, passed a few hours among them, he would have found they are not quite confined to the common beverage of whiskey. I never saw or heard of the heath, or such materials as he mentions, used in distilling spirits in any of those islands. Nothing is made use of but pure malt unmixed; and their spirits are, on these accounts, allowed to be superior in quality to any adulterated liquors elsewhere.

The lower order of people value themselves much on their connections with the rich. Connections often arise from the time that a mother, wife, or sister, gave suck to the gentleman's child; whence they call them *coalds*, co-fostered, or fosterlings. This appellation is used by all the family, as well as by the child whose mother's milk suckled the great man's child. This familiar epithet is no less useful to the rich than to the poor man; because, if the rich man countenances the poor, the last, in return, will think himself interested in protecting the flocks, and other effects of the rich; so that this tie of friendship being reciprocally useful, is continued for generations.

Most

Moſt of thoſe people are inferior to none in ſeafaring. From their infancy they are trained to it. Making of ſmall boats, with maſts, is the common paſtime of the children; and they are delighted with ſailing in boats when very young; but when they are able to handle the oars and ſails, they are truly active; and they ſeldom return home without fiſh, even when ſcarce on the coaſt. They never loſe ſight of their object either by night or day. Whether foul or fair weather, they are exerciſed when the fiſh is in great plenty, and if they had ſalt, with the proper implements for thoſe purpoſes afforded to others, their ſuperiority would ſoon become conſpicuous on that element.

But their genius is forced to run in an unnatural channel, by tying them down to work like ſo many negroes, with the whip ſmacking along their backs. They never will become dexterous at farming, that line of life being contrary to the natural bent of their inclinations.

The tenants repair to the hills all Summer with their cattle, and live in *ſhealings*;

that

that is, in huts, made in the hills for the Summer refidence of thofe who tend the flocks and herds. There the families live moftly on milk, butter, and cheefe, and fifh; and by the time they return to their farms, the grafs about their corn fields becomes excellent, and makes the cows yield plenty of milk. This is the cafe where the tenantry live comfortably under the protection of the proprietors, as they do in Lewis, and in fome inftances in the two Uifts; but cannot be fo much fo in Harris, becaufe all the horfes from the different iflands are fent to the King's foreft, where they devour moft of the grafs belonging to the back-fettlers, who border on this foreft; infomuch, that thofe people, in addition to their grievances, muft bear with this alfo; and their own corn, as well as grafs, is frequently deftroyed by numbers of hungry horfes. This is an intolerable grievance to thofe unlucky men; that they are often ftript of the fruits of their labours, without redrefs.

The poor tenants obferve the holidays about Chriftmas, and keep them very chearfully. Some of the humane tackfmen give them

them treats on one or more of thofe days, and fend for a mufician to make their fub-tenants happy. But the more modern incumbents drop thofe expenfive feafts, and their tenants may faft while thofe of others are feafting. Notwithftanding all the ill ufage that fome of thofe people fuffer, they bring their mafters the firft fruits of their own potatoes and meal from time to time, and fupply their tables alfo with fuch fifh as they can catch for their own families, beyond the rigorous extortions made upon them by paction. They take every method they can to footh thofe tyrannical people, in order to alleviate their own burthens, by their engaging manner towards their mafters.

## CHAP. V.

*Of St. Kilda.*

THE antient Herta at prefent belongs to the laird of Harris, and is known by the name of Saint Kilda. This ifland is fituated in the north-weft Atlantic Ocean, about 20 leagues fouth weft of Harris. It is about three miles in length; the foil fertile, the little valleys delightful, and the air falubrious and pure. There is an ancient fort in the fouth end of the bay, called Dunfir Volg. The arable land hardly exceeds eighty acres; but more might be added. Thefe produce plentifully, either corn, barley, or potatoes, and rye; of which the tackfman fhares liberally every year. The hills and pafture grounds are fully ftocked with cows, fheep, and lambs.

About twenty-feven families refide on this ifland conftantly; and are, perhaps, the

the moſt uſeful people on earth to enrich their maſter, by their induſtry in the fields, and their unrivalled alertneſs among the rocks.

The cows and ſheep are thought to be rather lower in ſtature here than in the adjacent iſles. The inhabitants are decreaſing in number from what they were in the end of the laſt century, being then one hundred and eighty in number; whereas in Mr. Macaulay's time (anno 1764) when miſſionary there, they decreaſed to about eighty. In Mr. Martin's time, their ſervice was much lighter, and their perſons leſs expoſed to danger among thoſe fatal rocks, in collecting feathers for their maſters. But their preſent maſter having forgot his former inſignificance, has aſſumed all the turbulent pride of a purſe-proud pedagogue, to keep them under.

There are four or five hills in the iſland, but Congara is, without exaggeration, the higheſt, and a real prodigy of its kind; it commands a tract of ſea and land more than one hundred and forty miles in extent. It

hangs

hangs over the sea in a most frightful manner: a sight of it from the sea astonishes, and from above strikes the spectator with horror. Its perpendicular height was found by Mr. Macaulay to be nine hundred fathoms. Few strangers will venture so near the edge of this stupendous precipice, as to look down to the sea immediately below them; yet the natives think nothing of it.

There are considerable hills in the small isles of Boreray and Soay, contiguous to St. Kilda, being about six miles distant, and these are fully stocked with sheep, and no small temptation for an avaricious master. Accordingly it is said, that those harmless people were forced to protect their flocks by force, about the beginning of this century, from their master, who demanded a sheep extraordinary from each family yearly; putting them in mind of a precedent of their having given an equal number to his predecessor. But they answered, that that was a voluntary gift, and on an extraordinary occasion, when he was wind-bound in the island, but was not to be a custom afterwards. However, the tacksman sent a considerable fiderable number of men to take them by force; but the natives armed themfelves with their fifhing and fowling implements, gave them fome blows, and forced them to retire, and would not pay that tax. By this ftout refiftance they preferved their freedom for that time: but alas! thefe days are now no more.

There is only one landing-place around all the ifland, and even there, except in a calm, there is no landing; while the reft of the ifle is furrounded by the moft tremendous rocks, hanging perpendicularly over the boifterous ocean; the moft awful that ever the eye beheld.

Thefe exalted rocks, in fpite of the terrible furges that frequently wafh their fummits, and make a noife like a perpetual roar of thunder, are neverthelefs more carefully divided among the inhabitants of this folitary ifle than their very corn fields.

This is the theatre on which they are moftly exercifed, and of courfe are beft acquainted there with, however awful and forbidding thefe precipices may appear to others. The moft of their time is employed among thofe clifts and coves, over all the faces of thofe monftrous rocks, in queft of eggs and fowls: the firft is ufed for their diet, and moft of the laft ftript of their feathers for their mafter's ufe. He makes a rich market of them at Liverpool, where they are fitted up for beds and other purpofes.

The art of the St. Kildians at catching fowls under the cloud of night is truly aftonifhing, and their fuccefs no lefs wonderful.

A man from that ifland told in a company where I was prefent, that he was one of the four men that catched four *itts*, or *pens*, being three hundred each, in the whole twelve hundred folan geefe, in one night. That bird, after the hard toil of the day at fifhing without intermiffion, rifing high in the air to get a full fight of the fifh that he marks out for his prey before he pounces upon it, and each time devouring it before he rifes above the furface, becomes fo fatigued at night, that he fleeps quite found, in company

pany with some hundreds, who mark out some particular spot in the face of the rocks, to which they repair at night, and think themselves secure under the protection of a centinel, who stands awake to watch their lives, and give the alarm, by *bir*, *bir*, in time of danger, to awaken those under his guard.

The St. Kildians watch with great care on what part of the island these birds are most likely to light at night: and this they know by marking out on which side of the island the play of fish are, among which the geese are at work the whole day; because in that quarter they are ready to betake themselves to sleep at night. And when they are fairly alighted, the fowlers repair to the place with their panniers, and ropes of thirty fathoms in length, to let them down with profound silence in their neighbourhood---to try their fortunes among the unwary throng.

The fowler, thus let down by one or more men, who hold the rope lest he should fall over the impending rocks into the sea, with a white a white towel about his breaſt, calmly ſlides over the face of the rocks till he has a full view of the centinel; then he gently moves along on his hands and feet, creeping very ſilently to the ſpot where the centinel ſtands on guard. If he cries *bir, bir,* the ſign of an alarm, he ſtands back; but if he cries *grog, grog,* that of confidence, he advances without fear of giving an alarm, becauſe the gooſe takes the fowler for one of the ſtraggling geeſe coming into the camp, and ſuffers him to advance. Then the fowler very gently tickles one of his legs, which he lifts and places on the palm of his hand; he then as gently tickles the other, which in like manner is lifted and placed on the hand. He then no leſs artfully than inſenſibly moves the centinel near the firſt ſleeping gooſe, which he puſhes with his fingers; on which he awakes, and finding the centinel ſtanding above him, he immediately falls a fighting him for his ſuppoſed inſolence. This alarms the whole camp, and inſtead of flying off they all begin to fight through the whole company; while in the mean time the common enemy, unſuſpected, begins in good earneſt to twiſt their necks, and never

gives

gives up till the whole are left dead on the spot.

This goofe is almoft as large as a land goofe, of a white colour, except the tops of the wings, which are black, and the top of the head, which is yellow. The bill is long and fharp-pointed, extremely hard, and pierces an inch deep into wood. There is an Act of Parliament againft the cruel manner of faftening herring on planks far out at fea, to catch thefe darling geefe, and a fevere penalty againft tranfgreffors of this inhuman act. A well fupported fact concerning the ftrength of this fowl, is told by one of the tackfmen of this ifland. Once when failing towards St. Kilda, and entering upon a field of fea where the geefe were bufy darting among the fifh, from on high, on each fide of the large barge in which he fat, and failing faft before the wind, the barge paffed over a fifh fo quickly that a goofe who had marked it out, and rufhing fo violently through the air, inftead of the fifh, on account of the unforefeen accident, darted his ftrong bill quite through the barge, and was actually carried back to Harris dead, with his bill
through

through the plank, as a teftimony of the fact.

The nefts of the folan geefe, not to mention others, are fo very clofe, that when one walks between them, the hatching fowls, on either fide, can always take hold of one's clothes; and, fays Mr. Martin, will often fit ftill till they are attacked, rather than expofe their eggs to be deftroyed by the fea gulls. Their mates furnifh them with food while they hatch.

The feafon for catching the old folan geefe, is before they begin to lay. About the middle of May is the time of gathering their eggs.

The young folan geefe are larger than their mothers before they begin to fly, being extremely fat. That on their breaft is very deep. The greafe is kept in bags made of the ftomach of the old geefe. They call it *giban biurtach*. They have never but one egg at a hatching, in any neft at St. Kilda. They lay again, and even a third time, if deprived of the firft egg. The gulls have

more

more at a time. The folan goofe can carry five herrings at a time to his mate or young, and fpue them out of his gorget in the neft. This fowl digefts fo quickly, that inftances are given when the bird was fhot immediately as he appeared above the furface; and the fifh was found half digefted in his ftomach, that was juft devoured below.

The Fulmar is highly efteemed among the St. Kildians, for its many good qualities; for they think the world cannot produce any thing to equal it in value. The fulmar furnifhes oil for the lamp, down for the bed, the moft falubrious food, and the moft efficacious ointment for healing of wounds; in a word, fays the poor St. Kildians, deprive us of the fulmar, and St. Kilda is no more.

This fowl lays no more than one egg in a feafon; the leaft offence makes her quit her neft, fo nice are her feelings, and therefore it is a high crime in St. Kilda to plunder its neft of the egg.

The

The young ones of this species are in season in August. The moment he is attacked in his nest, he squirts the oil in their faces; therefore the fowlers surprise him, to preserve the oil. It is thought that the fulmar picks its food from the fat of whales, or other fat fish, because of such quantities of oil, perhaps a quart or two at a time, which the natives preserve when they catch the young by surprise, not only for their lamps, but also as a catholican for diseases, and have used it for that purpose. The fulmar is a grey fowl about the size of a moor-hen. It has a strong bill, with wide nostrils. It sits on the rock, when the wind is to blow from any quarter, and it is said to be a certain sign of westerly wind when it goes to sea.

The Lavie is another species of the St. Kilda birds. These visit the island in February, being the first that appear in the season. The people congratulate each other on the auspicious presage of their approaching happiness. At this time they settle the operations of their campaign, and divide their people into parties.

This

This bird refembles a duck, though rather longer; lays its eggs on the bare rock, and if not carefully touched, they tumble in great fhowers over the rocks. Sometimes one man catches four hundred lavies before he touches the rope to haul them up. After thefe are hauled up, the adventurer alfo is hauled up, and is highly praifed for his activity.

This fowl fupplies the wants of the St. Kildians when their frefh mutton is exhaufted. Then the folan goofe is in feafon; after that the puffins, with a variety of eggs; and when their appetites are cloyed with this food, the falubrious fulmar, with their favourite young folan goofe, (called *Goug*) crowns their humble tables, and holds out all the Autumn.

In Winter they have a greater ftock of bread, mutton, potatoes, and fallad, or *rifted* fowls, than they can confume. In fpite of their hard ufage, they enjoy more human felicity, than any fmall or great nation of flaves, in St. Kilda, though the deareft place on earth.

The

The puffins hatch under ground, and are eafily found out by a hole dug by their beaks. They have dogs trained up for this purpofe: thefe are a fpecies of terrier or fpaniel. The women are much exercifed in fowling; and the dogs find them out, and bring the birds of their own accord to the tops of the rocks.

The people live all Summer on two kinds of thefe puffins; for there are more forts of them than one, and fo numerous, that they not only cover whole plots of ground; but when on wing, they cover every thing below them in a kind of darknefs, like a fmall cloud of locufts in another country.

At St. Kilda there is a large kind of fea-gull, called a *Fuilag*, as large as a folan goofe, that infefts the birds by breaking their eggs, often killing the young, and many of the old fowls. Thefe good-natured people difcover their greateft rage, at feeing or hearing of this cruel enemy; they exert their whole addrefs to catch it, and then excell the Indians in torturing this imp of hell. They pluck out its eyes, few its wings together,

and

and fend him adrift. They extract the meat out of its egg, and the animal fits on it till it pines away. To eat its egg would be accounted flagitious, and worthy of a monster only. This fowl is white in the breast, black in wings, and blewish on the back.

The Gare Fowl is four feet long, and supposed to be the pigeon of South America. Its egg is said to exceed that of a goose, as much as the latter exceeds the egg of a hen, which it lays close by the sea-side, being incapable from its bulk of soaring up to the clifts. It appears in July, and even then but rarely, for it does not visit St. Kilda yearly.

Fowls are also caught by gins; and Mr. Martin mentions one extraordinary escape, when he visited that island. One of their number was entangled by one of his own gins: when his toe got into the noose, he fell down the rock, and hung by the toe, the gin being strong enough to hold him for the space of a night twenty fathoms above the sea, until a neighbour heard him, and rescued him next morning.

They

They have been known to preserve two thousand solan geese, young and old, all Winter, in their store houses, of which they have scores, for keeping their fowls and eggs. The least of their baskets will contain four hundred eggs; and they have been known of a morning to have brought home twenty large baskets full from the rocks; and many of them will hold eight hundred eggs of lesser size. Instead of salt they use peat ashes for preserving their fowls and eggs. These are unpleasant to such as are unaccustomed to eat of them, being generally too harsh to the taste.

Their village is placed on the east side of the island of St. Kilda, which they call their country, and the little isles of Boreray and Soay are named the north country. Their houses are low, and flat roofed, and the avenue between them is called the high-street. They have nitches made in the sides of their walls, about five feet from the ground, to sleep on; and instead of feather beds they use straw or heath. As they keep their cattle's dung in their houses, as in Harris, placing one stratum of earth well tramped with fresh litter below their cattle, the floor and fire are raised about

about five feet above the ground by the time this augean ſtable is cleaned out in Spring.

Theſe are a few of their ſingular methods of catching birds among the rocks, and to ſuch as would ſee them perform within the walls of gentlemen's houſes, their alertneſs is no leſs aſtoniſhing than diverting, when they ſcramble along the ceilings; but it is terror itſelf to look at them among the clifts at this diverſion. A clergyman of my acquaintance was witneſs to two noted bird-catchers among the ableſt of them, and was almoſt terrified to look down at them. One fixed himſelf on a craggy ſhelf, his companion went down ſixty fathoms below him, and having darted himſelf from the face of one of the moſt tremendous rocks, he began to play his tricks, ſinging and laughing very merrily; but ſo terrified was the clergyman, that he could not for his life run over half the ſcene with his eyes.

After playing all the antic tricks and entertainment of his art, he returned in triumph with ſtrings of fowls about his neck, and a number of eggs in his boſom. The people

people were inexpreſſibly happy, but the miniſter was extremely ſhocked at this uncommon trial of ſkill.

The man who holds the rope plants himſelf ſo firmly on a ſhelf of the rock, that he has been known to ſuſtain the other, after falling the whole length of the rope.

Theſe people for certain excell all the people in Britain at climbing. It happened once that their boat was ſplit to pieces on the weſt ſide of Boreray Iſland; and they were forced to take hold on a bare rock, which was ſteep, and above twenty fathoms high. Notwithſtanding this difficulty, ſome of them climbed up to the top of the rock, and let down a rope from thence, with plaids, to draw up all the boat's crew; a circumſtance incredible to ſtrangers, and impoſſible to any but themſelves to ſurmount. In this iſland they were forced to remain until the ſeaſon returned for their oppreſſor to viſit the iſle for his dues; and that only happens twice a year. Let any man of reflection conſider the wretched ſtate of theſe men, without food, fire, or cover from the wintry blaſt, during

the

the long nights—with the unhappy situation of their poor forlorn families at home, not knowing but their hufbands, parents, and brothers, had been fent to eternity; and who, though within fix miles of St. Kilda, were deprived of a fix fhilling Norway yaul to go in queft of them, dead or alive.

Melancholy were their looks, when their lordly mafter carried them home.

How cruel and impolitic does the heritor of this ifle behave to thefe brave men!

The imprudent part of the laird's conduct lies in not placing thofe under his own protection, as other tenants, and receiving his rents from themfelves. In that cafe, inftead of eight, or even ten pounds yearly rent, he might be in the receipt of more than double that fum. One half of the dues paid annually by the tenants to the tackfmen, would enable them to live with more comfort to themfelves, and greater advantage to the laird. Then they could join in a large barge, and repair to markets with their goods, and enrich themselves with their unrivalled induſtry. We have ſeen part of their labours and danger, and we ſhall by and by remark, how they are rewarded by their maſters for whom they riſk their lives daily.

Out of eighty acres of land they muſt pay fifty bolls of barley and potatoes yearly; and he keeps his own dairy-maid on the iſland to receive every drop of their milk to make butter and cheeſe for ſupplying his own table; this muſt be carefully collected evening and morning; and the remainder he ſends to the market. The high price of feathers, and the immenſe quantities collected by theſe people, increaſe the tackman's income immenſely. All this, with the barley and potatoes, for the trifle of eleven guineas rent yearly; to which ſheep and lambs muſt be added. According to the laws of this land, every houſeholder muſt pay to the perſon he calls his maſter, every ſecond he lamb, every ſeventh fleece, and every tenth ſhe lamb. Theſe ſheep are wonderfully fruitful, many of them having four, and often three lambs at a time; as one of the people aſſured my friend,

friend, Mr. Macaulay, that in the courſe of thirteen months, one ſheep increaſed his flock with nine more; the ewe brought forth three lambs in the month of March, three more in the ſame month the next year after; and each of the lambs had one before they were thirteen months old. Yet in proportion to the number of ſheep every man poſſeſſes, he muſt pay this heavy tax, which becomes very profitable to the tackſman, but proportionably iniquitous and oppreſſive to the poor ignorant St. Kildians, who muſt bear their own country acts, many of them unknown to their lairds, and almoſt all of them to the laws of this realm.

Well, indeed, might a certain gentleman who viſited St. Kilda, declare that all their cattle are more beneficial to the maſter than to the people—for having an old preſcriptive right to their milk from May to Michaelmas, and, I am afraid, to the end of time, theſe people will be at the mercy of ſome tackſman or other.

Though the infamous pot-penny and fire-penny are dropt, as the people have got pots and flints of their own, yet there may

be

be many other mean practices exercised over thofe harmlefs people, without their having an opportunity of conveying thofe grievances to the ears of the public, with whom they can have little intercourfe. However, the above is no flender fpecimen of their bad ufage.

As no ftranger failing by, ever ventures to land on this boifterous ifland to barter with the natives, they muft be fupplied with all marketable neceffaries from their mafter's fhop. And one may eafily conjecture on which fide the balance lies, on thofe occafions.

The people of St. Kilda, from the nature of their food, emit a difagreeable odour. Fifhes in general abound with much oil, and are often rancid on the ftomach, and affect the very fweat with a difagreeable fmell, that offends the olfactory nerves of delicate conftitutions; and no wonder, though thofe water-fowls that daily feed on fifh, fhould partake much of the fame tafte and fmell—and this is particularly the cafe of the folan goofe, whofe flefh taftes exactly of fifh.

The

The men and women here are more chaste than those of Harris are known to be.

The women are more handsome, as well as modest; they marry young, and address strangers with profound respect.

Both men and women delight much in singing; and their voices are abundantly tuneful. Their genius and natural vein for poetry is no wise inferior to the other natives of the Hebrides. Their songs are wonderfully descriptive, and discover great strength of fancy. The subjects of their songs are the accomplishments of their fair friends among the female sex; and the heroic actions of their fowlers in climbing rocks, catching fowls, and fishing, and melancholy deaths over the rocks.

The men there, as in Harris, sing aloud when tugging at the oars, and exert their lungs and strength in animating the party by their united iorrams in the chorus of these songs, which are adapted to the business in hand.

They are not addicted to the vice of drinking, so detestable in others. That article of luxury is wisely kept back from them: as intoxication, from their dangerous profession, might soon unpeople the island. The men and women are equally ingenious; the women at weaving webbs, and the men at other handicrafts. Being there strangers to the superfluities, they rest satisfied with the common necessaries of life.

The men and women dress in the same form that the Hebrideans do, and are possessed of an equal share of pride and ambition of appearing gay on Sundays and holidays, with other people.

Their language is Gâlic, unadulterated, having no communication with strangers, to corrupt it with other languages.

Buchanan writes, that in his time the inhabitants of Herta were totally ignorant. But the proprietor sent a priest along with his procurator yearly to baptize their children, and in the absence of the priest every one baptized his own child; often their midwife

wife performed that ceremony. In this ſtate the people continued for a hundred years after, until an ignorant fanatic impoſtor groſsly imposed on the people, by claiming tythes; but a part of them refuſed to pay that tribute, alledging he was unqualified for the profeſſion, as he could not repeat the Lord's Prayer.

Fifty years after his time, another dangerous impoſtor formed a deſign of raiſing a little ſpiritual empire among them: his name was Rore, and he had penetration enough to find out that ignorance was the mother of devotion.

This native of Herta, though ignorant of letters, had great natural parts. Full of his own abilities, he laid a deſign of enſlaving the whole community, and making himſelf lord of their conſciences, freedom, and fortunes.

He impoſed a falſe religion on them, which he pretended he had been taught by John Baptiſt, and in his prayer he ſpoke of Eli as their preſerver, and maintained he met with
him

him on a fertile little hill, which he called his bush, which was sacred, and any cow or sheep that would taste of its grass was to be instantly killed; of which he himself behoved to share liberally during the feast. He taught that each of them had titular saints in heaven to interceed for them, whose anniversary behoved to be kept by a splendid feast for each; and that Rore himself was to be partaker. The women were all brought to his creed, and a criminal prosecution was instantly begun against any who was hardy enough to oppose him, by making them walk over a large beach of loose round stones, without moving them, which would truly be a great miracle, as the stones are round and loose. In case, however, a stone gingled, her punishment was, to stand naked under a cataract and a mighty torrent of water, let down with great force upon her head and body. Private confession was his great engine, and the greatest secrecy was enjoined, under the pain of hell fire.

But he was at last, with great intreaty, enticed on board a vessel, and carried to Sky, where he made public confession of his crimes,

crimes, and was never allowed to return to St. Kilda.

These people at present profess the Protestant religion. Their clergyman is illiterate, farther than his little knowledge of the English language. At St. Kilda he studied his divinity from his father, who was a poor man that failed in his circumstances, being a farmer and mechanic in Uist, before he was clothed with the character of a minister, and was sent to officiate among those people; in which capacity he continued till his death opened the vacancy for his son, who was judged qualified to explain the English Bible into Gâlic.

The salary annexed to this office is about twenty-five pounds per annum, being mostly a mortification of three hundred marks left by a gentleman of the name of Macleod, to be given to any name-sake, who can answer the above purpose; and the rest to be made up by the Society for propagating Christian Knowledge in Scotland; as no man of letters would be buried from the world for

such

such a small sum. He acts up to this duty to the best of his knowledge.

This island will continue to be famous, from its being the place of imprisonment of the Hon. Lady Grange, who was, by private intrigue, carried out of her own house, and violently put on board a vessel at Leith, unknown to any of her friends, and left her great personal estate in the possession of that very man who entered into this horrid conspiracy against her; he sent her to this wild isle, where she was barbarously used, and at last finished her miserable life, among those ignorant people, who could not speak her language.

A poor old woman told me, that when she served her there, her whole time was devoted to weeping; and wrapping up letters round pieces of cork, bound up with yarn, and throwing them into the sea, to try if any favourable wave would waft them to some Christian, to inform some humane person where she resided, in expectation of carrying tidings to her friends at Edinburgh.

This

This affair happened about the year 1733, owing to some private misunderstanding between her ladyship and Lord Grange, whom she unfortunately married. But the real cause continues a secret, since her ladyship never returned.

This shocking affair would never have been heard of from that quarter, where secrecy is reduced into a solid system of dangerous intrigue, against residing, but unconnected strangers, had not her ladyship prevailed on the minister's wife to go with a letter concealed under her clothes all the way to Glenelg, beyond all the Isles, and deliver the letter into the post-office, where it found its way to her friends. They immediately applied to Parliament, to make enquiry into this barbarous conspiracy; and though a vessel was fitted out from Leith immediately, yet it was supposed a courier was dispatched over land by her enemies, who had arrived at St. Kilda some time before the vessel. When the latter arrived, to their sad disappointment, they found the lady in her grave. Whether she died by the visitation of God or the wickedness of man, will for ever remain a fecret: as their whole addrefs could not prevail on the minifter and his wife, though brought to Edinburgh, to declare how it happened, as both were afraid of offending the great men of that country among whom they were forced to refide.

Some people imagined, that fhe knew fomething of the rebellion that broke out in 1745, at that time, and meant to have divulged the fecret, which is not very probable.

CHAP.

## CHAP. VI.

*Modes, Implements, and general State of Huſ-bandry, in its rude and natural Form.*

THE general manure of the land is ſea-ware, either cut with ſickles, or caſt on ſhore by the violence of the ſurge. All over the two Uiſts, and the low lands, as well as the iſles about Harris, the carriage of the manure is generally performed by horſes, or, where theſe cannot travel, on the backs of men and women. The furniture of the horſes is a kind of rope made of benty graſs, which is brought round a wooden ſaddle, called a cart-ſadle, under the animal's belly. Over this frame are hung a couple of panniers, or creels. The wooden ſaddle is farther ſe-cured by a kind of crupper, from three to four feet long, brought round from either ſide of the girth under the horſe's tail. A band

band tied tight around his lower jaw supplies the place of a bridle. Three or four of those horses, and sometimes greater numbers, are tied to one another's tails. Some of the gentlemen have begun to introduce carts, which will greatly lessen the number of small horses that have hitherto been thought necessary on farms.

The severe carriage of manure for the land in Spring, and of kelp in Summer, wears out the horses: supplies of which are brought every year, into the other islands of the Western Hebrides, from Lewis.

In the back settlement of Harris, men, women, and children, must be constantly under the panniers, as no horse could be of much use there, where the men can hardly walk with their loads.

One must be a hard-hearted taskmaster that will not pity a poor woman with her petticoats tucked up to her knees, and a heavy load of dung, or wet sea-tangle, on her back, mounting those rugged declivities and steep hills, to the distance of a compleat mile

mile from the sea before they lay the burdens on the ground. The men work, with skins above their coats under the panniers, and their short sticks in their hands: and neither frost nor snow, wind nor rain, will make them quit their labour till night, when once they are begun, and thoroughly wet.

Their being obliged to use the tangle where the sea casts it on shore, and the grounds nearest the sea being exhausted, is the reason why they must often mount very high up the faces of those horrid mountains, where very little earth is to be found among the craggy rocks; and they are therefore obliged to collect earth into small spots, by way of ridges. Those little collections are called *feannags,* and the furrows between their ridges or feannags are generally six feet wide; while the strip of a ridge is often less in breadth; because of the want of earth in some parts, and of the depth of the moss in other places. The furrows in the one case must be also deepened three feet, and the ridges in proportion raised above the water. That of the other is widened, to collect the little earth into a ridge. This renders the whole

whole back fettlements of Harris almoft impaffable, as a man meets conftantly with feannags, and wide furrows to leap over. And indeed travelling through parts of Uift alfo is dangerous to ftrangers, becaufe large white fields of dry fand, as far as the eye can reach, refembling new driven fnow in whitenefs, and driving acrofs the paths, infomuch that new foot-paths are made daily, without any vifible elevated objects to be directed by, one is generally bewildered. This is the cafe all over the immenfe plains of white fand left by the ebb, called fords, where the paths are always wafhed away, and no vifible object to direct by. A ftranger, on this account, without a guide, is almoft fure of lofing, not only his way, in going acrofs thefe broad plains, but alfo his life. In the hills, and in the northern parts of Harris, there are pillars here and there erected, and ftones placed on the top of rocks, where travellers muft make a ftretch to pafs through thefe zig-zag paths by their direction; otherwife the natives may lofe their way, as well as ftrangers. It is, therefore, abfolutely neceffary to have fkilful guides when travelling over either countries.

Figure

Figure out to yourfelf one of thofe ridges covered over with thick fea-ware; and a man cutting the fward of the furrow with a fpade, (*cafs direach*) and a woman up to the knees in that quag-mire before him, lifting up every turf he cuts, and covering the ware with them, all over the ridges. You fee the conftant labour of both the fexes, while the fpots on the different places where the tangle is to be found, remain unfinifhed. From this little fketch of their daily labour through Winter and feed-time, in preparing the ground for the grain, with cutting and carrying the fea-ware and horfe dung to the fields, I refer to any man, whether the five fhillings a year for wages are not laborioufly earned, even though they were not to refund little damages. Some of the tackfmen are fo inhumanly rigorous, as to deprive the poor people of their miferable pittance, under that pretence: others, with all their feverity, keep none of their little earnings back. Frequently, indeed, their wages do not amount to five fhillings: unlefs they are the principal fervants, they have ftill lefs.

The sea-ware will make any soil produce luxuriant crops of barley and potatoes, but the oats do not succeed so well by far over the country, as the grain is generally small. The great oats have been tried without success, as they soon dwindle down into small grain. The laird of Boisdale has tried wheat with success, and his knowledge in farming makes the deep moss carry a sward equal to any loamy soil. The sea-ware has commonly the effect of making the deepest and coldest moss keep a firm sward, even when applied by men whose judgment in farming is by no means of the first rate.

The cattle of every kind descend from the hills to feed on the sea-ware in Winter; and after they have filled their bellies, they return to the heath to mix that dry substance with the grass and heath, to qualify each other. The inhabitants must be very careful of their goats, which, when neglected, are often drowned on the little rocks by the tide, as they are bad swimmers. Instinct leads them down as well as the other cattle, when the ebb begins; yet they have not the same sagacity to retire in time.

The

The little old Scotch plough is quite simple, and has a fock and coulter, with two handles almoſt like the Engliſh plough, drawn by four little horſes; but ſo weak, that another kind of a ſimpler plough, called the *ruſtle*, with a crooked iron reſembling a hook, paſſing through a ſtick of four feet long, and drawn by one horſe, cuts the furrow before that drawn by four horſes, to make it eaſy for that plough. *Cromman-gadd* is a ſimpler plough than the old Scotch, and drawn by two or more little horſes. It has only one handle, and the ploughman goes with his left ſide foremoſt. The *caſs chrom* is a kind of plough ſomewhat like a ſpade, that is only driven by men's feet. The head of this plough is four feet long, with an iron ſock, and with a handle of ſix feet long, that is faſtened in the head with a peg for the man's foot to puſh it under the furrow, which is turned as well as with the other plough. Before this the *ruſtle* muſt cut alſo. The *caſs direach*, or ſtraight ſpade, is commonly uſed for cutting the turf on the top, or trenching, which a woman or man lifts and places it on the ridges, above the ſea-ware. This is called, in their language, *taomadh*.

When

When they want, by cutting out of the middle of the ridge, to spread it toward the sides, they call it *taomadh a broin*. This last operation is necessary when the crown of the ridge becomes too sharp, in order to make it flat. When the corn is sown on the ridge they harrow it, (one harrow, drawn by a rope or thong, is fastened to the tail of the horse) but very frequently it is only raked.

The potatoes are planted in beds, by placing the seed above the dung or sea-ware, and covering them, as already observed, out of the furrows, by the hands of a woman or man, as they do when the *taomadh* for the barley is made as already mentioned, or by a dibble, in case the *taomadh* has been made some time before, and the holes filled with the rakes.

They never reap their barley, but pluck it by the root; and after it is stacked, and fit to be dried, they cut off the roots for thatch. But the oats are cut with sickles, and the grass carefully shaken out of every handful, lest the sheaf should be long a drying.

The

The grafs for hay is commonly cut with fickles, from the left to the right, contrary to the manner of cutting corn in England, and the fouthern and inland parts of Scotland.

The crop is carried on the backs of horfes, where they can be ufed, and upon the backs of men and women, where the horfes cannot work. Their ftacks are built moftly conical, every row being bound faft with heather ropes from the bottom to the top, and they are covered with no thatch through the Winter.

Their flail confifts of a hand-ftaff and a fhort thick fupple, either of wood, or tangle, bound to the ftaff by a thong, fix inches diftant. With this implement dangling round their right arm, they thrafh the oats and barley. They never fwing the flail round their head; nor ftand upright at this work. The women are generally employed at thrafhing, efpecially among the poorer farmers, while the men are at the mafter's work, or fome where elfe ufefully employed. The ftraw is carried to the fields for gentlemen's cattle, who are feldom houfed, but fed in good Winter grazing, (called *geary geambry*) and

and those are much stronger and bigger than the poor tenants cows, which must be housed, as they have no Winter grass on the fields for them. And the prices of each are vastly different, as the gentleman will sell a cow at four guineas, while the poor man will be glad of the half, and seldom draws so much from the drovers.

The Winters are seldom so severe in those islands as on the continent of Scotland. The snow lies but a short time, and not very deep. On that account their cows are able to stand the Winter. Their yearlings must be housed, and fed with hay or straw, in the same manner as the poor men's cattle are, being as yet not hardy enough to stand the Winter blasts.

Their kilns are but small; nor do they spread the barley on the surface above the straw to be dried. They cut the heads of the barley, and lay them in order upon the bare ribs. When they are dried, they are hauled down on the floor, and immediately thrashed, and winnowed, and clapt up hot in plates, ready for the quern. So that a

man

man can cut the sheafs dry, and thrash the barley, clean it for the quern, and make his breakfast thereof after it is ground.

The tenants make sieves of sheep-skins, and sift the meal on plates made of grass, or on large goat-skins placed on the floors. This is done evening and morning, when they quern as much grain as their diets require.

Horses and cows were formerly the staple trade of these isles, and they have raised the prices of both wonderfully of late from what they were formerly. Now kelp has taken the precedence; an article some years past unknown over all these countries. And no country whatever can vie with them in the quantity and quality of that kind of commodity, particularly over Lewis, the southern isles of Harris and Uists. So that in proportion to its extent, no country in Europe can equal it in point of riches, which are yearly drawn from the vast droves of cows, horses, sheep, and goats, that are exported, besides the much larger store of wealth which the kelp and crops raise. These

com-

commodities are increafing both in value and in quantity; for the kelp grows thicker by cutting it oftener.

This ware is cut with fickles every third year, for kelp, and the immenfe quantity of caft ware, or tangle, which hurls daily on the fhores for the fame ufe, bring very rich returns from the markets to the owners yearly. We obferved already, that this ware is immediately carried from the fea to fpread on the fields to dry, either on the backs of horfes, or of women.

The kelp kilns are from eight to twelve feet long, and three feet broad. After one floor full is burnt of the kelp, or ware, two men work the red-hot liquid with irons made for the purpofe, until it becomes hard; and then they burn another ftratum above, and the fame operation is gone through, until that alfo is hardened into a folid body, and fo on from one ftratum to another. And then it is well covered with turfs, to keep out the rain, until a veffel arrive to carry it to the markets.

This

This is the hardeſt labour which the people have throughout the year, and at the time they are worſt fed; becauſe their own potatoes, or little grain, are, by this time, moſtly conſumed. The oat-meal, by them called the white meal, or *min bhan*, by way of diſtinction from the graddan meal, which is blackened by the ſmoke and aſhes of the ſtraw, being purchaſed, is very ſparingly dealt among the people, that if poſſible, they may not eat more of it than the price given them for making each tun of kelp can afford: and thus, inſtead of paying part of their rents with their Summer's labour, they may ſink deeper into their maſter's debt.

Lord Macdonald deals on very liberal principles with his kelp-makers. They are well fed, and therefore can ſave a part of their gain; but ſuch as have run in arrears with the tackſmen, are miſerably ill off. They are obliged to ſtraiten their belts very conſiderably: and in theſe times hunger is written in legible characters in the face of the wretched labourer.

This

The nature of this work requires their attendance by night and by day, frequently, in fome of the remote little ifles, where even the flender affiftance of their poor families cannot reach them with (*wilks*) periwinkles, or any kind of fhell-fifh. Such poor men as thefe can hardly afford to keep a milch-cow: fome of them have two ewes, bound together by a rope called *caiggean chaorich*, to give a little milk for the poor ftarved children at home; but of this luxury the father of the family cannot then partake; and they are frequently obliged to kill thefe milch-ewes for their food, when their families are at the point of ftarving.

When the cuddies, or other fifh, happen to be on the coaft, thofe poor men make a kind of livelihood; but when they are not, their cafe is deplorable---one while at the kelp, and immediately thereafter running to the fhore for wilks, oyfters, clamy fifh, *crechan fhell-fifh*, or any that can be eat, to quiet a hungry ftomach. The meagre looks and feeble bodies of thefe belaboured creatures, without the neceffary hours for fleep,
and

and all over in dirty ragged clothes, would melt any but a tyrant into compaffion. Yet if any quantity of their fet compliment of kelp remains unfinifhed, the deficiency muft be accumulated to their former debts, to make up the pretended lofs of the cruel man.

It is truly mortifying to find a people naturally induftrious, altogether crufhed. The poor women are at the querns, or baking cakes, long before day-light, and all the while finging with furprifing fpirits.

When they are making peats, five people are employed. One cuts the peat; another places it on the brink of the ditch where it is dug; a third fpreads it on the field; a fourth pairs and cleans the mofs; and a fifth is refting, and ready to relieve the man that cuts. And thus the round is taken by turns. The women are feldom at this work, but the men help one another alternately; fometimes they muft reft fatisfied with fewer hands; but the above is the full compliment required to perform the work, according to their tafte.

They

They take the corn to the open fields to winnow; becauſe their little barns, if they have any, have no back doors to open, to let in the winds. The better ſort have ſmall doors within their barns, to receive the wind from the different quarters; ſtill, however, the fields are moſtly uſed.

CHAP.

## CHAP. VII.

*Of Marriages, Baptism, and Burials; with the several singular Ceremonies and Usages.*

MARRIAGES among the gentlemen are attended with no greater pomp than among the better fort through Great Britain; they are commonly attended by their friends, who make merry on the happy occafion. Contracts are only known to few. But it is not fo with the common people. They invite the friends on both fides, to make up the contract of marriage; and as all the poor people retain that part of their former importance that entitled them to the honour of gentleman (*duinne uafle*), at leaft in words, it is fuppofed that the lady's parents will not make a trifling offer of portion to their intended fon-in-law. A pompous promife, if they fail in the performance, adds much to the dignity of the match. Being prefent at one of thefe meetings of friends, I obferved that the friends of the young man began with a fet fpeech, by informing the parents of the caufe and defign of their meeting, which was, to pave the way for an alliance with the family to which the woman belonged; and then launched out at confiderable length on the great and good qualities of the young man who afpired at the connection. Meanwhile, they remarked, that the friends of the gentleman were fuch as ought not to be received with indifference. It ought, they proceeded, to be efteemed a very happy turn of Providence to caft fuch a hopeful youth and good friends to back him, to folicit their friendfhip. They hoped, therefore, they would make an offer of fuch a portion to the young woman, as might do honour to themfelves, and worthy of fo promifing a young man.

The portion formerly was paid in cows, fheep, and goats, thefe being more valuable to them than money; and this old practice is continued in full force. Even if the parents fhould have none, they muft name a
number

number of cows, and a handfome number too, otherwife the young man would think his dignity fuffered in the eyes of the neighbours. Twenty cows are among the moft moderate portions promifed, and many of them confiderably above that number. If the young couple had reafon to be fatisfied with each other during the courtfhip, the affair is generally fettled to the fatisfaction of the parties, after which they begin to make merry. They eat, drink, dance, and fing, &c. &c.

But as their cows are but few, they muft take, at the time of payment, a kind of reprefentative value of it. Accordingly I was told that a year old cow ftood for one; three ewes for another; a fpinning wheel for a third; two blankets for a fourth; a fmall cheft for a fifth; and fo on until the number agreed upon was compleated.

On the Saturday evening after the contract is fettled, their names muft be given to the parifh clerk to have the banns publifhed in the church the following day. This piece of ceremony they are truly averfe to, as

private

private marriage is more eligible, and they wish much not to have their names called. They pretend to be ashamed on these occasions: but I believe the true cause is the fear of alarming others of the sweet-hearts, who might step forward to claim a *prior* right, and perhaps occupancy. I myself have seen the proceedings stopped by the opposite party, while the publication of the banns was going forward.

However, when there is no interruption made, they appear before the clergyman, when the ceremony is regularly performed. After the ceremony is finished, the parson calls to the bridegroom to remember his duty to the bride; and as an earnest of obedience to his reverence, the swain gives her a hearty kiss. A very rough scramble follows among the other men, who try which will have the good fortune of getting the next kiss from the blushing bride: after which she is led home in triumph, with a large bag-pipe playing some chearful march, and other tunes composed for the purpose.

One

One would naturally wonder that women of eafy virtue, as we before defcribed, fhould not find it difficult to meet with helpmates: yet fo it is, that many inftances can be produced, when the men ftrive to get their favourite in fpite of what may be alledged againft her virtue.

They make large weddings, and they frequently fpend more money than their promifed portion on the occafion; though they fhould want in the after part of life. It is cuftomary for both the bride and bridegroom, juft before their marriage ceremony, to untie their fhoes, garters, and fome other bandage, to prevent witchcraft, of which they are much afraid on thefe occafions, and think this an antidote againft it.

In many parts of Scotland a practice prevails, which not only leffens the expence of the weddings, but even makes them fo profitable as to enrich the young couple. That is what is called *penny-weddings*, at which the bridegroom prepares a feaft, and invites the whole country. Every man, and every woman,

man, pays a fhilling, which, voracious as they may be, is twice as much as the value of what they eat. The men drink four or five fhillings a-piece, fo that (to fuch poor people) a great fum is collected. Thefe penny weddings, and all promifcuous meetings, it is faid, contribute much to population.

Their baptifms are accompanied with ceremonies that are innocent and ufeful, for cementing the peace of the country, more efpecially among themfelves. Baptifm is adminiftered either in public or in private;--- juft as it fuits the conveniency of themfelves and their minifter. After this the parents prefent the child to fome neighbour, and call him *gofti*, or god-father; and after kiffing and bleffing the child, the *gofti* delivers the infant to the mother, and ever afterwards looks upon himfelf as bound not only to be careful of that infant, but alfo very much attached to the parents. They call one another *gofties* during life. This name becomes more familiar to them than their own Chriftian names.

Nay,

Nay, if they had formerly been at variance, by this fimple union they become reconciled to one another. They never come to the minifter, without a bottle of fpirits, and are commonly merry on the occafion.

Burials are preceded by the large bag-pipe, playing fome mournful dirge. They continue playing till they arrive at the place of interment, while the women fing the praifes of the dead, clafping the coffins in their arms, and lie on the graves of their departed friends. It is common to fee women coming out to ftand by the way-fide, who are ftrangers, as the corpfe is carried along, with certain mournful ditties in their mouths, and making great lamentations; while they in the mean time afk fome of the attendants where the corpfe came from, and whether they are men or women.

On thofe occafions, there is great profufion of meat and drink brought to the place of interment, where the expences generally bear a proportion to the rank and fortune of the perfon deceafed, to prevent the imputation of meannefs; and they feldom feparate
while

while the cafk contains any fpirits to wafh down their forrow: which feldom happens before their griefs are converted into fqabbles, and broken heads, which fome of them carry home as marks of remembrance for their loft friends.

They feldom difplay much mirth at late-wakes,* as they do in many parts of Scotland; but fit down with great compofure, and re-hearfe the good qualities of their departed friend or neighbour. Their grief foon fub-fides after they are buried; and many have fpeedily replaced a loft wife by fome of their former acquaintance.

* In many parts of Scotland it is cuftomary for the youth of both fexes to fit up by the corpfe, and confole themfelves by whifkey and other paftimes.

CHAP.

## CHAP. VIII.

*Oppreſſive Cuſtoms----Tenants foſtering their Maſter's Children without Board Wages---Begging of Cows, Sheep, and Goats, after Marriage---Begging of Wool---Begging of Cocks---Anecdotes.*

THE tackſmen ſend their children to be foſtered among their vaſſals. There are ſeveral pernicious cuſtoms that prevail among the better ſort of tackſmen, to diſtreſs the poor tenants, unknown in other countries. By ſuch infamous means, they become at once poſſeſſed of no inconſiderable ſhare of the wealth of the poor inhabitants.

The moment that the child of a great tackſman is nurſed, the moſt ſubſtantial of the ſubtenants is pitched upon as the moſt proper perſon to foſter the child. And this the
tenant

tenant muft look on as a piece of great condefcenfion in the mafter; and no inconfiderable mark of honour and refpect done to himfelf, to be thus entrufted with fo precious a charge. And from the moment the child is conducted to his houfe by a fervant, he is dignified with the appellation of *eddigh*, and his wife with that of *muimmé*: a ftepfather, and ftep-mother.

By this diftinguifhed character, each are addreffed thereafter. The child never fpeaks to them but by that venerable name; nor they in return, but by the title of child. And this child is not only well fed and clothed by the *muimmé*, but fhe alfo muft attend the *daultidh*, with more care and attention than any of her own, that the parents, of any of them, may have no reafon to complain that their child is neglected in meat, clothing, or cleanlinefs.

By the time that this *daultidh*, or ftepchild, is ten or twelve years old, and generally well foftered, the parents carry him or her home, to fend them to their education: and inftead of paying any board wages for
all

all this expence of meat and drink, conſtant attendance, and clothes, for the child, it will be all loſt labour, unleſs their *daultidh* is accompanied home with a preſent of cows, ſheep, or goats, and clothes, in proportion to their reſpective abilities.

And the foſter-father and mother are always more or leſs reſpected by the true parents, in proportion as they continue to load their ſtep-child with preſents. The moment they fail in that part of their duty, then they are allowed to paſs along in the common crowd of beggars, hardly noticed by the ſtep-child or parent.

In this, as well as many other particulars, I am not likely to avoid the imputation of being too ſevere, or departing from the truth. I muſt here, therefore, as in former circumſtances, be excuſed by the kind reader for proving my allegations by teſtimony.

One Monro, called Macandy, was a rich ſubtenant, under different great tackſmen; and his wife nurſed children for them all; and from his kind attention to his *daultidh*,

was

was truly honoured and efteemed, nor, to fay truth, is there a more lady-like woman, without difparagement, in all Harris, than his wife was, and ftill is, for her age.

It is commonly the cafe in this unfortunate country, that though a man is poffeffed of feveral hundreds of fheep in the foreft (becaufe in this place they are not reftricted by their mafters from multiplying their flocks) when he begins to fail in ftrength, he is in a fhort time ftript of his property, and becomes a beggar.

But this was not the whole of the cafe with Macandy; for he had not only great flocks of fheep roaming through the hills, but a vaft herd of cows, and a good farm, with money at intereft in his mafter's hand, whofe benefit it was to continue fo wealthy a tenant in one place unmolefted. Befides, he alfo foftered the prefent tackfman (who is now a full Captain in the Army) which ought to entitle him to double care and attention in his old age, from his fofter-fon. This man alfo is in poffeffion of the money that the foſter-father was poſſeſſed of, as ſucceſſor to his father.

What, then, was the conſequence of ſo much expence and tender care? Why the foſter-ſon left the foſter-father and mother, both blind with age, being one hundred years old, without a leaſe, and at the mercy of a ſteel-bowman that hardly has an equal for ſeverity; who made old blind Macandy and his blind wife pay equally dear for leave to ſit and lie in a hut, while any of his cows, ſheep, or horſes remained, as the youngeſt and ſtouteſt of his ſcallags: obſerving, that though he foſtered his brother-in-law, that was nothing to him. Thoſe poor aged blind people at length were reduced to apply for their money to pay their rents; but as money lent by ſubtenants to their maſters, is ſeldom returned, Macandy applied for his money in vain: in vain even to the lady to whom he delivered his money, and whoſe ſon he foſtered, and in whoſe poſſeſſion her bill acknowledging the receipt lay. Macandy finding that all his good deeds were thus repaid, gave his bill to his foſter-ſon's agent and relation, being alſo no inconſiderable confiderable limb of the law, in expectation of receiving payment through his hands, as he is a manager of the rents, as well as a lawyer: but there alfo he has failed. As it is not intended to pay up the money, excufes are eafily invented.

Thus I have feen the aged pair blind, and feeble with age, fitting or lying in their hut, without cow, fheep, or goat, or bread, to fupport them, but what the charitable poor fubtenants fent to their huts, as they are unable to take up their beds on their backs (as other beggars muft) to walk about the different bays, to be maintained.

There is a very charitable gentleman in London, who in his younger days remembered to have feen Macandy, not only fervant to his father for years, but alfo a wealthy tenant. This gentleman, from compaffion, ordered a certain quantity of meal to be given them yearly, after he heard of their diftreffed circumftances, and has alfo applied for the bill, that he might make the money be forthcoming: but as he is in earneft determined to force them to give up the money so justly due; others are as much in earnest to defeat his intentions, and therefore he will never come at the said deed.

One Macdonald, *Callum M'Innish*, a more respectable character still than old Monro, who fostered another son to this singular family, fared worse still; for, along with fostering the child, they sent their servants to work in his neighbourhood, and because he refused to feed them with the milk of his own cattle, he was instantly obliged to betake himself to the King's forest with his family and cattle, and even to carry their own son with him to this asylum, and to keep him for years thereafter, even though he never returned back to their lands more: nay, after the boy was at Stornaway town, at school, where he died, Malcolm was sent for, and had to hire men and a boat out of his own pockets, to carry the corpse to Roudle to be buried, a space of fifty-six miles, in a severe storm, in Winter; while the parents only took the trouble of meeting the corpse of their own child, as others of the neighbours, after the poor man was at all this expence and trouble.

This

This is another inftance, and only one of the many peculiar to this famous family, of parental affection for their children; and alfo points out their power, like the Centurion; " They are men in authority, and can fay to one man, go, and he goeth; to another, do this, and he obeys it." Nay, one Ruaridh Macilphadrick, who was once richer than both the former put together, and foftered many of thofe children, yet is now not only a common beggar, but unfortunately deranged in his faculties, and cannot finger one fhilling of the fums of money he lodged in the hands of a tackfman, whofe word he depended upon without a bill. And though he fays, that the fon knows of this, and knew the confidence he placed in the father's honour, ftill he refufes to pay a farthing, becaufe he had not fecured a bill. It is in vain for the aged man to reply, that bills were not neceffary in thofe days, when a man's word was deemed fufficient; but times are altered.

This fhameful practice is too common to be refuted; and, if it was attempted, the men are ftill living teftimonies of the facts:
how-

however surprising the narrative may appear to people of more free and liberal sentiments.

Another shameful practice commonly exercised to fleece the poor in this country, is the mode of going round the whole tenants over the parish to beg for cows, sheep, and goats, after marriage, under pretence of stocking a farm.

The moment a gentleman, in possession of a farm fully stocked, with all its compliment of cattle, thinks of marrying a woman, whether his fancy lights on the daughter of a rich or poor man, a stranger or native, be he old or young, rich or poor, himself, the new married woman loses no time to go the round, accompanied by the man and maidservant, to try her fortune among the wretched tenants, under pretence of stocking the farm.

It is expected, on those occasions, that every one will deal liberally to the kind lady that did them the honour of standing under their roof. Immediately a runner must

muſt be diſpatched for a ſheep or more, as their reſpective circumſtances are ſuppoſed to admit of, that *bean-n'tighe*, the good wife, may be preſented with them to ſtock the farm ſhe is entering upon.

Each of theſe ſtrives who ſhall receive moſt, as by this mark of attention a proof is given of their eſteem to herſelf, and as it points out the rank that the family ſhe belongs to holds in the eye of the common people. And ſhould any ſturdy ſtubborn man prove churliſh on thoſe important occaſions, he might have occaſion to repent of his refuſal; and therefore when hardly (*a caigean*) two ſheep for giving milk to their children remain, yet they are cautious of refuſing *bean-n'tighe*.

Thus every new *beann*, or good wife, like a new broom, ſweeps almoſt clean before her, and leaving behind only a houſe full of ragged hungry children crying for meat, with the mother and father to divert them.

I am aware, that it may be obſerved, that it is not peculiar to the Weſtern Iſles, for perſons

persons to go about their neighbours, to procure additional stock to their farms. In various parts of Scotland, young beginners make a circuit through the country, soliciting donations of corn, potatoes, hay, and straw. That practice, which is called *thigging*, is very different from the one which we are describing. The former makes the humble supplication of poverty, the latter the exaction of arbitrary power. Here, indeed, as elsewhere, the poor are obliged to solicit chariatble contributions of corn, potatoes, and other articles of subsistence. The tenants themselves, experienced in distress, are prone to succour the miserable.

But those poor people, who are liberal to the rich, must be extremely cautious how they venture to pray them for assistance. Some of the rich make it a rule to grant no relief; but to dismiss from their gates unhappy persons who owe their abject state to their oppression.

The young are easily initiated in the principles of rapacity and tyranny, which so uniformly regulate the conduct of their parents.

In the beginning of Spring, the young gentlemen go about among the tenants to collect their cocks and hens. As the parents extort their quadrupeds from these oppressed people; so do the children the bipeds. They carry their servants with them, and force the tenants to part with great numbers. They pretend that they want them for fighting; but in reality convert them into money; and often sell them to their owners themselves. Should any subtenant refuse to give his fowls, or an equivalent, the parents will find means to make him regret his resistance to the insolent exactions of youthful tyranny. Perhaps, the young despot himself would, on the spot, inflict punishment on the audacious rebel, who should have the presumption to maintain his own rights.

Thus fleeced by the extortions of their superiors, the poor people are moreover exposed to the importunate solicitations, and demands of their equals, from the neighbouring isles. Swarms of the wives tenants of Uist, and the small isles, come in Summer to the hills of Harris to spunge on the poor inhabitants, to get presents of wool

wool and clothing. Each of thofe begging females muft have a fervant to carry the bags of wool which fhe collects. A dozen of them is often quartered on a poor tenant in a night. One of the family, the next day, accompanies them to a neighbouring farm, *monftrator et comes hofpitis*. The ftrangers carry their diftaffs and fpindles along with them, and fpin as they proceed, and when they fit down to reft. As they are engaged in their own work, and are fed by others, they make their circuit at their leifure. The expence of thofe vifitors, added to the rapacity of the tackfmen, compels the poor tenants to be half naked, and half ftarved, even in the coldeft weather; and when engaged at the hard labour before defcribed.

It will naturally occur to the reader, that the gifts to the mendicant females are voluntary, and confequently not grievous. In fact, though nominally voluntary, they are really compulatfory. The mendicants, have eafier accefs to their landlords and landladies, frighten them with threats of complaints. They even come often reinforced

inforced by the recommendations of the tackſmen's wives, or ladies, (as they ſtile themſelves) which the tenants dare not diſregard. Here, indeed, as in all countries where arbitrary power prevails, oppreſſive as the ſupreme deſpot may be, a great part of the ſuffering of the ſubjects ariſes from ſubordinate tyranny.

I have heard the practices of proprietors in former ages adduced as a precedent for burdening the tenants with the maintenance of their children, and expecting from them preſents of cattle with them when they returned to their parents. Such a practice, indeed, prevailed. The favourite vaſſals being of entruſted with the heir, and other children of the chieftain, always ſtrengthens their attachment to the intereſt of the family. But the conduct of the chieftains in former times, and of the tackſmen in the preſent, was very different. The proprietor protected the benefactors of his children, and gave them long leaſes, and additional farms, and did every thing in his power to promote their advantage. Benefits conferred on the generous gentleman exacted gratitude, and procured
friend-

friendſhip and patronage. Preſents conferred on illiberal avaricious tackſmen, only increaſe rapacity and cruelty. Where generoſity ought to prevail, not even juſtice takes place. Inſtead of gratitude, come inſolence, injuſtice, and barbarity.

## CHAP. VIII.

*Anecdotes of Prince William Henry—Of the Town of Stornaway, in Lewis----Contraſt between the Dawnings of Liberty and Comfort opened in Lewis, and the preſent State of the adjacent Iſland of Harris---Former Manners and Mode of Life in the Hebrides compared with the preſent.---A Compariſon of the Condition of the Hebrideans, and other Highland Scallags with that of the Negroes in the Weſt-Indies---Obſervations on the Attempts to introduce extenſive Fiſheries into the Iſlands and Highlands of Scotland.*

From ſcenes of oppreſſion and ſorrow let us now turn our eyes to the dawnings of liberty and comfort introduced into that portion of the Weſtern Hebrides, that has fortunately fallen into the poſſeſſion of the Hon. Mr. Mackenzie of Seaforth; whoſe
genius

genius and purfuits may be confidered as
characteriftical, in fome meafure, of the
prefent age, when the falfe glitter of barbarian war begins to give way before the real
fplendour of humane philofophy: a noble
and elevated mind, inftead of purfuing military renown under the banners of fome unjuft and ambitious conqueror, employing
his time and talents in the acquifition of
knowledge, and the application of knowledge to the ufeful arts, and the increafe of
human happinefs. This modern ULYSSES,
inftead of wandering from his ITHACA, like
a neighbour of his, in order to acquire fortune and fame by arms, in diftant countries,
remains at home, the guide and the father
of his people.

The chief town in Lewis is Stornaway.
It is with equal commodioufnefs and elegance laid out in regular buildings and
ftreets. The merchants have built excellent
peers and quays, for loading and unloading
veffels, of which there is a great refort. The
bay in which it is fituated, is fafe, and the
harbour fpacious and eafy of accefs; with

excellent

excellent ground for anchoring. Here is excellent accommodation, and good entertainment, at moderate rates, for ſtrangers, in public houſes and coffee-rooms. The private houſes of the merchants and tradeſmen diſplay neatneſs, plenty, and a kind, as well as elegant hoſpitality; being plentifully ſupplied, by means of their home and foreign markets, with all the neceſſaries, and even luxuries of life. Stornaway, ſeparated by its ſituation, from the main land of Scotland, but approximated to various commercial towns, by eaſy water-carriage, is not confined to the Celtic cuſtoms that prevail in the Highlands and Iſlands in general, but readily adopts the modes of the capital, and the improvements of every country.

This town, a few years ago, was honoured with a viſit by Prince William Henry, when he made a voyage and tour through the Hebrides. Travellers, with very few exceptions, never think of voyaging through the Weſtern Hebrides, or touching on the Long Iſland; but paſs on by Sky, Mull, Tyree, Iona, and Coil. Prince William took a wider a wider range. And as the Prince performed a more extensive voyage in those parts, than our common travelling antiquarians, and botanists; so he was more curious and minute; and perhaps, more judicious in his enquiries, which did not so much relate to insects, shells, feathers, and druidical remains, and those *lusus naturæ*, those whirligigs of Nature, that so much attracted the attention of a certain Welsh traveller, as to the civil and political state of society; the domestic situation of the people; and the state of the useful, or mechanic arts. He conversed with freedom and affability, through an interpreter, with the lower orders of the people, enquiring into their situation, occupations, and manner of life. He condescended, wherever he touched, to carry along with him many pieces of workmanship peculiar to the Isles, and which displayed, though ruder than the handicrafts of manufacturing countries, the contrivance and invention of the natives; and what their genius, with proper cultivation and encouragement, was capable of producing. A very different opinion was formed of those genuine remains of the ancient Celts, than

that

that which is profeffed by the Goth, Pinkerton, who thinks that the Highlands of Scotland will never flourifh in ufeful or liberal arts, till the Celts be driven or otherwife removed out of it; who calls them CATTLE, and fcarcely allows them to be of the human fpecies. But of this gentleman, and his noftrums and animofities, I fhall take an opportunity of faying more in another work of a more comprehenfive nature and extent than the prefent, which I intend, God willing, in the courfe of a year, perhaps lefs, to give to the public.

Prince William, whenever he took a fancy to any thing, always made a very princely return, which, with the frank manner that accompanied it, made the hearts of thofe poor people, fo little accuftomed to the favours or condefcenfion of their fuperiors, leap with joy. It is fuperfluous to fay, that the Prince is beloved and adored among a people oppreffed by tyranny and cuftom, yet fenfible by nature, and ductile and open to every impreffion of gratitude. The Prince, as may eafily be fuppofed, was received in Stornaway with the utmoft refpect, and honoured

by

by all poffible attentions; and he was highly fatisfied with his reception.

The merchants of Stornaway, among other branches of commerce, deal deeply in the fifhing trade. Several of them employ one, two, or more veffels, in the proper feafon, conftantly on the look-out for herrings. Their fituation is very happy for fifhing, being near to the weft fide of Lewis, and thofe lochs and weftern coafts, which are reforted to by the deep fea herrings much more than the eaftern fhores either of the main land of Scotland, or of the neighbouring iflands. The gains of the adventurers are, *communibus annis*, confiderable on the trade; and they draw a large portion of the royal bounty for the encouragement of the fifhery. They alfo fend great quantities of oil, feal-fkins, and other fkins, annually to the markets. The Stornaway fifhers, ftill farther, have become famous for the vaft herds of porpoifes which they kill in their lochs, fometimes by hundreds at a time.

Trade, but chiefly the fifhing trade, gives birth to a lively fermentation of general induftry, duſtry, not only in Stornaway, but in other parts of Lewis; where the natural activity of the inhabitants is farther encouraged by the wife and liberal policy of Mr. Mackenzie, in conſtructing roads, and by juſt regulations, leaving to the induſtrious the reward of their toil. Stornaway is a market, and is daily becoming a greater market for the produce of the foil, and the fruits of the fold and field. In the town of Stornaway there is a growing demand for houſes; the building of which gives employment to many hands; as maſons, carpenters, ſmiths, day-labourers, &c. and people to cut, dry, and bring home peats, of which the conſumption is daily increaſing. Such a lively little town cannot but be a ſource of ſatisfaction and pleaſure, as well as of advantage to the lord ſuperior of whom the inhabitants hold their tenements, who is an eye witneſs of their induſtry, and ever ready to encourage the introduction of whatever may tend to the general improvement. How happy a change has been brought about in the iſland of Lewis ſince the reign of James VI. of Scotland and Firſt of England, a period of leſs than two centuries! That Prince, who

was

was a great encourager of all the arts of peace, fent a colony of induftrious fifhermen from the fhire of Fife, in Scotland, with feveral Danes and Dutchmen, to teach and to exhibit an example of ufeful induftry to the natives, with the encouragement of large allotments of bays, and lands indifputably in the gift of the Crown. The heir to Macleod, the chieftain of Lewis, together with his neighbours, fell upon the unfortunate ftrangers from the low-lands, and maffacred them to the number of many hundreds in one night. The prefent chieftain of Lewis feems ftudious to expiate the barbarifm of his predeceffors.

A very different face of affairs from that which we have juft been contemplating in Lewis, takes place in the neighbouring ifland, or rather peninfula of Harris, and for the moft parts in all places in the Hebrides, where the people are not under the eye of fome great and liberal lord, whofe mind and fortune confpire to nourifh liberal ideas in his breaft, and to diffufe comfort all around him. On a general furvey of the weftern Hebrides, as we have feen, the picture that is ofteneft

ofteneft prefented, and which recurs again and again to the mind, is that of melancholy and depreffion. Thofe ifles are, in general, the melancholy abodes of woe, of fuffering in various forms, where the people are treated merely as beafts of burthen, and worfe than beafts of burthen. If want and ftripes leave any room for fenfibility to a ftate of flavifh dependence and cruel revilings and mockery, furely the tears, the cries, the groans, of fo great a number of oppreffed, though lively and acute people, call for pity and relief at the hands of Government!

The public attention has of late years been called to the fituation of the African cultivators of the foil in the Weft-Indies. God forbid that I fhould infinuate a difapprobation of any mode of conduct, whofe object is mercy. Let me, however, obferve, that there are certain divifions, claffes, and tribes of men, that have a claim to our fympathy and aid, in preference to others; both by the laws of natural, and thofe of revealed religion: and, having made this obfervation, let me inftitute a comparifon

of

of the African in the West-Indies with that of the Celtic slave or scallag in the Western Hebrides, in the neighbourhood of Luskintire in particular.

First, then, with regard to the respective conditions of their life, in general, it is none of their own chusing. The African, when he is not sold on account of some crime, is bereft of his freedom, and forced into slavery by fraud or violence. The Hebridean slave is neither, indeed, trepanned into slavery by guile, nor compelled by physical compulsion; but he is drawn into it by a moral necessity, equally invincible; by a train of circumstances which are beyond his power to control; and leave him no option, but either to serve some master as a scallag, or often to protract a miserable existence for some time, in the forest, and near the uninhabited sea-shores, where he may pick up some shell-fish, to perish, with his wife, perhaps, and little ones, through cold and hunger.

Second. With regard to labour. The negroe works only from six o'clock in the morning to six in the evening: and out of that time he has two complete hours for rest and refreshment. The scallag is at work from four o'clock in the morning to eight, nine, and sometimes ten in the evening.

Third. With regard to respite from labour. The negroe is allowed only one day in the week for himself. And this, too, is the portion of time allowed to the scallag.

Fourth. With regard to food. The negroe has a plentiful allowance of such common fare as is sufficient to nourish him; besides his little property in land, or *peculium*, which he cultivates for himself, on the evenings, after he is done his master's work; and on Sundays, and other holidays. The scallag is fed only twice a day, when at hard labour for his master, with water-gruel, or as they call it, *brochan*; or kail, or coleworts; with the addition of a barley cake; or potatoes: and all this without salt. But, for his family, and for himself, on Sundays, or when unable to work through bodily indisposition, he has no other means of subsistence than what he can raise for himself by the labour of one day out of seven,

from

from a scanty portion of cold and moorish soil :---Barley, potatoes, coleworts, and a milch cow, or a couple of ewes, perhaps, for giving milk to his infants: though it often happens that he is obliged to kill these household gods, as it were, in order to prevent his family from starving. At certain seasons, he has fish in abundance; but this he is, for the most part, obliged to eat without bread, and often without salt. The negroe, if he be tolerably industrious, can afford, on Saturdays, and other holidays, with pepper-pot, a pig, or a turkey, and a can of grog. Nay, many a negroe, I am well assured, has been known to clear, besides many comforts for his own family, by the produce of his little property, from twenty to thirty, and even forty pounds a year: so that there is a fair probability, that any negroe would soon be enabled to gain the price of his liberty, if he desired and deserved it. Of relief from bondage, and woe, the scallag has not a single ray of hope on this side of the grave.

Fifth. With regard to lodging and clothing. The negroe is comfortably lodged and fed

fed in a warm climate: the scallag is very poorly clothed, and still more wretchedly lodged, in a cold one. And, as the negroe is provided by his master with bedding and body clothes, so he is also furnished by him with the implements of husbandry. The scallag, with sticks and sods, rears his own hut; procures for himself a few rags, either by what little flax or wool he can raise; or by the refuse or coarser parts of these articles furnished by his master: and provides his own working tools, as the spade, called *cafs direach*, the *cafs chrom*, &c.

Sixth. With regard to usage or treatment. The slave is driven on to labour by stripes, so also is the scallag; who is even, as we have seen, formally tied up, on some occasions, as well as the negroe, to a stake, and scourged on his bare back. The owner of the slave, it may farther be observed, has a strong interest in his welfare: for if he should become sick, or infirm, he must maintain him; or if he should die, he must supply his place at a considerable expence. There is no such restraint on the peevish humours, or angry passions of a Hebridean laird

laird or tackſman. The ſcallag, under infirmity, diſeaſe, and old age, is ſet adrift on the wide world, and begs from door to door, and from iſland to iſland. Nor is it neceſſary, in order to ſupply the place of a ſcallag, to be at any expence : for the frequent failure of ſubtenants affords but too many recruits to the wretched order of ſcallags.

Seventhly, and laſtly. As there is nothing ſo natural as the love of liberty, and an averſion to reſtraint and oppreſſion, the ſcallag, as well as the negroe, ſometimes attempts emancipation, by fleeing to the uninhabited parts of the country: though ſuch attempts are not ſo often made by the ſcallags after they are enured to ſlavery, as when they feel themſelves on the verge of ſinking into that dreadful and deſerted condition of exiſtence.

The only aſylum for the diſtreſſed in the Long Iſland is the King's foreſt : where ſeverals are ſheltered with their families and cattle for the Summer ſeaſon; where they live in caves and dens of the earth; and ſubſiſt, without fire, on milk, the roots of the earth, and shell-fish. But in the Winter season, cold and famine drive them back again to seek for subsistence and shelter under the same tyranny that had driven them to the forest. The blue, and other mountains, afford the means of life to runaway negroes (if they can escape the searches of their masters) both Summer and Winter.

In the West-Indies, no planter, or captain of a vessel, is allowed, by the law of the Colonies, to kidnap, conceal, or keep any runaway slave, or, by any means, to detain him from his master. Here, also, the comparison holds between the slave and the scallag. There is not a tacksman who will take or retain in his service, or on his land, either the scallag or subtenant of another master, without a written certificate from that master, that the scallag or subtenant has a good character; and also, if he be otherwise satisfied as to the character of the poor man, that his master is willing to part with him. For as the colonists, by their laws, so the tacksmen of the Western Hebrides, by their country regulations, have
entered

entered into a firm compact, that no one shall harbour the subtenant or scallag of another, who does not produce a proof of his humble and unlimited obedience to his former master. Now, it is evident, from reason, were it not proved by experience, that certificates are most withheld where they are most wanted. For, no landlord who is known to be cruel to his people, will ever give them certificates; because in that case they would all leave the tyrant, and seek for milder treatment under some less severe master. Certificates of good behaviour are very naturally required with servants: but neither is it possible, for all masters and mistresses to combine in a system for enslaving poor servants; nor in England, does the humanity of the law leave the poor without redress if they did: for, by the late excellent law, respecting masters and servants, the latter can claim a certificate, if the former cannot shew just cause for refusing it.

As I had not entered into the tyrannical combination among the tacksmen, I ventured to engage in my service a young man, of whose good behaviour I was well ascertained,

tained, but who had not a certificate from his former mafter. But I was foon obliged to give him up. His poor parents were fubtenants to that mafter: who quickly conceived the idea of ufing them as hoftages for the humble return of their fon. Thofe poor people were informed, without ceremony, that if he did not immediately return to his labour, they would be fharply looked after, to teach themfelves and their children better manners in future. Accordingly I parted with him.

I am told that there have been many inftances of a cunning clever flave having found ways and means to get quit of his mafter, not only by fleeing into the back or hilly country, but through the contrivance of fome charitable failor, who has concealed him under the hatches, until he efcaped out of the ifland, and fo regained his liberty.

There are inftances too, of poor men, by fimilar methods, making their efcape from Harris, and other parts of the Long Ifland. I have known young fellows, who had imprudently married before they were well able to build a hut for themſelves; and of their going, from a terror of falling at that early period of life into the condition of ſcallags, on board ſome fiſhing veſſel, on pretence of lending a hand for a few months in fiſhing, and taking the firſt opportunity of making their eſcape at Greenoch, Port Glaſgow, or any other port where the veſſel put into: thus leaving their families to the mercy of their maſters.

An old but active man, whom I knew, Evan Macleiſh, a ſubtenant to the miniſter of Harris's father-in-law, by bribing a ſailor, made his eſcape with a concubine and her three children, (whom he had kept for years under the ſame roof with his lawful wife) below the hatches, unknown to the captain of the veſſel, ſafely to Greenock.

One would imagine that Macleiſh, who had been ſo long indulged by his maſter in living on his ground according to his own taſte, might have truſted to him for continued friendſhip. But notwithſtanding this ſpiritual indulgence, he had but little hope that the miniſter would ſhew him any forbearance

bearance in temporal concerns. Forefeeing that, fooner or later, all that he had muft become the property of his mafter, and he himfelf a fcallag, he chofe to tranfport himfelf with his concubine, and her brood, while he had the means: leaving his old wife behind him as a legacy to the minifter and the parifh of Harris.

It has been recorded by different writers, that among the Norman pirates, there were many who had never flept, for a courfe of feveral years, in any houfe where there was fmoke: and, not very far back, one Reginaldus, of Norman defcent, a great chieftain of the Hebrides, lived in the fame manner; accuftoming himfelf to all manner of hardfhips.

It is alfo reported of one Bredan More *Na-b'Uaii*, fuppofed to have been the father of the Macdonalds, that when he made an irruption from the Hebrides into any part of the main land of Scotland, he commonly lodged with a thoufand men, in a large cave, in a rock, called, in the Gâlic language, *Uaii Bhridean:*

*Bbridean:* and that thofe hardy iflanders lived on venifon, fifh, milk, whey, and the roots of the earth; with very little ufe of fire.

So natural is the love of liberty, that I verily believe, what I have been affured of by many a poor Hebridean, with tears in his eyes, that thoufands would prefer the fame kind of hardy and wild, but independent ftate, to the condition of fcallags and oppreffed fubtenants, were it permitted to them. Yes, they would willingly live on fifh, and vegetables, with a little fea-water, perhaps, condenfed, and rendered more falt, by means of evaporation, even without potatoes; provided they were allowed to fhelter in fome hut raifed by their own hands, near the fea-fide; but this privilege they are not allowed, unlefs, together with the fpot for building a hut on it, and a garden for vegetables, they alfo take a piece of moffy ground along with it, that may effectually by the tenure of holding it, in fact fubject their perfons, and all they have, to the will of the landlord.

No human condition is abfolutely happy or independent. There is a mixture of mifery in every lot: and all men (as is juftly obferved by a certain refpectable writer on the fubject of flavery *) are more or lefs dependent on one another. There is a mutual connection and fubordination, that runs through the whole family of mankind, from the fceptre to the fpade, from the king on the throne to the peafant attached to the foil. Whether we have refpect to former or prefent times, we fhall find that a very great majority of the human race have been, and now actually are, in the ftate of bondmen and bond-women, to fuch of their fellow-men as were deftined by Providence to move in a higher order in political fociety. As there are gradations in animal and intellectual nature, fo alfo there are gradations in human fociety. Such, in reality, is the actual fituation of human affairs: fuch the oeconomy of Providence. And why fhould there not be divers ftations, as well as divers orders of beings? If it be fit that there
fhould

---

* William Innes, Efq. of Lime ftreet Square, in the City of London.

should be men as well as angels, why, in like manner, should there not be bondmen, and bond-maidens, as well as princes and princesses, kings and queens? The minds of men are fitted by education and by habit for the different states and stages of society, in which they exist. The advancement of tribes and nations of men from rudeness and ferocity of manners, to civilization and liberty, must be gradual. Sudden transitions from one state to another, like convulsions in the human frame, agitate society, and endanger its existence. It is by a meliorating change in men's minds, not by the operation of sudden and violent laws, that either nations or individuals can pass from vice and barbarism to virtue and refinement. Changes more sudden and decisive would only tend to derange the order in which human affairs naturally proceed; and, by prolonging the reign of confusion, anarchy, discord, and barbarity, to prolong also the misery, together with the excessive inequality of mankind. The truth of all this is emphatically illustrated by what has passed, and is still passing in our day, in Russia.

The

The Czarina, willing, on her acceſſion to the Imperial throne of Ruſſia, to raiſe the peaſants attached to the ſoil to the condition of freemen, inſerted in her new code of laws a clauſe for effecting this object in a very rapid manner. But it was ſoon found neceſſary to eraſe this clauſe for the peace and ſafety of the nation. The barbarous Ruſſians, knowing as little bounds between liberty and licentiouſneſs, as between a reaſonable ſway and deſpotic rule, abandoned themſelves to the moſt infernal intoxication and exceſs; and had they not been reſtrained within their uſual folds of fixed cuſtom, would have proceeded, as ſome of them in fact did, and many of them threatened, to a general maſſacre of their lords, and univerſal devaſtation.

The preſent Archduke of Ruſſia was induced, from the nobleſt motives, to manumit all the peaſants on one of his eſtates, by way of experiment, how far he might venture on the ſame meaſure in others. The peaſants were put in poſſeſſion of the ſtocks on the different farms, and thenceforth to pay certain fixed rents for a limited term of years,

years instead of personal service. They were at first infinitely delighted with their new situation.—They reaped the harvest, abandoned themselves to drunkenness, and sold all the produce of the soil, without even leaving seed for another crop. They fell of course into extreme misery, and unanimously joined in a petition to the Archduke, which was readily granted, to be taken under the charge of their former overseers, into their former servile situation!*

I entirely agree in opinion with this gentleman. That there should be different orders or conditions of men, is agreeable to the plan of Providence; and not superseded by that of grace. *Onesimus* was acknowledged to be the bond-man of *Philemon*, at the same time that he was admitted to a participation of all the privileges and hopes of Christianity. I also readily allow, that in order to the emancipation of slaves, it is necessary,

in

---

* Mr. Innes informs us that these instructive and interesting particlars in the modern history of Russia, are given on the authority of Mr. Swinton, a near relation of the Russian Admiral Greig, who has lately published his Travels during a course of three years, in Russia, Norway, and Denmark.

in the firſt place that they be made capable of being good members of ſociety: that their minds be freed before their bodies. But after they are by education in the Chriſtian Revelation, like the poor *ſcallags*, humanized, enlightened, and raiſed to the ſpiritual converſation, views, and hopes, to keep them in a ſtate of ſlavery, has in it ſomething that is monſtrous and ſhocking. The Danes, after they had carefully inſtructed and trained up their negroes, in their Weſt-India ſettlements, in the principles of morality and the Chriſtian religion, and experienced their good behaviour, generally gave them their liberty, even before the late Daniſh law for the gradual abolition of ſlavery, and received, in the increaſed induſtry of the well-tutored and free ſervant, a full recompence for the liberality of their conduct.

There is no law, it is true, authoriſing ſlavery in the Hebrides: but the ſcallags are ſlaves *de facto*, though not *de jure*. I wiſh, therefore, that ſomething might be done, by the wiſdom and humanity of the Legiſlature, for their relief.

Mr.

Mr. Burke, who feems to think that this world was made only for gratifying the luxurious appetites of a few great ones, obferves, with regard to the poor, that they have the confolations of religion. True: yet, it is natural for them to avoid, if they could, hunger, nakednefs, and oppreffive labour in this life. What, it may be faid, can the Legiflature do? Shall they make a law, that no laird or tackfman fhall keep a *fcallag*? No. This would be as abfurd, and cruel, as it would be to enact, that no Weft-India planter fhould keep an African flave: in both which cafes the poor wretches muft ftarve. But open a field of induftry, and let the door of this field be open to every one who chufes to enter.

The natural refource of the maritime and hardy inhabitants of the Weftern Hebrides, far advanced in the northern and deep feas, is fifhing: an occupation to which they are, as we have feen, much addicted. But the lairds and tackfmen, as we have alfo feen, will not fuffer them to fettle even in huts on the fea-fhore, unlefs they become, in fact, their

their predial flaves, by taking a piece of cold wafte land.

Certain patriotic Scotchmen, the Duke of Argyll, Lord Breadalbane, Mr. George Dempfter, and others, moved by thefe confiderations, have fet on foot a fcheme for introducing liberty, with induftry, among the poor Highlanders and Iflanders, by fetting free fome fpots of ground from the grafp of tyranny, there raifing the ftandard of liberty, and inviting the induftrious to come thither from all quarters as to the abodes of freedom, where they might be fecured in the poffeffion of quiet and independent habitations. Certain fifhing ftations have accordingly been fixed on; where the Britifh Society encourage fettlers, by the conftruction of harbours, roads, warehoufes, with neceffaries and implements for fifhing on reafonable terms, and permament *domicilia* to them, and theirs after them. All this has a tendency, no doubt, to nourifh and ftimulate a fpirit for fifhing. And it is to be regretted, that the fifhing ftations were not either made more numerous, or more happily chofen. They lie all of them, except that in Lewis, on, or in the iflands adjacent to, the main land of Scotland; where there is neither fuch plenty, nor large and ftrong fifh, as live in the deep feas, and are occafionally driven into the lochs and bays on the weftern fide of that chain of iflands which compofe the Weftern Hebrides, and are known, more commonly, by the name of the Long Ifland. On that fide of the Long Ifland, the beft, beyond all doubt, for fifhing ftations, there has not fo much as one fuch ftation been chofen by the Britifh Society; and on the eaft, in Lewis, only one. It is not every one, indeed---it is but very few of the poor working people in the Long Ifland, that can afford the expence of tranfporting themfelves and their families, and fixing themfelves in the fifhing ftations in Sky, Loch Broom, Cannay, Rafay, and Oban; but were they only permitted to have a permanent habitation on the fhores of the lochs and bays in their neighbourhood, and with which they are acquainted, where fhoals of herrings croud annually; and the fineft cod, ling, haddocks, whitings, &c. are to be had at all times for the catching, this mere permiffion miſſion would ſow the ſeeds of induſtry, in the way of fiſhing, all over thoſe remote iſles, more effectually than the greateſt bounties, or common conveniencies. There has been, of late, a great deal written againſt exceſſive monopolization of land;* and, with much reaſon. If ever there was a neceſſity, or propriety in eſtabliſhing agrarian laws in any part of the Britiſh dominions, it is in the Highlands and Iſlands of Scotland; and eſpecially the chain of iſles called the Long Iſland: where the land is, for the moſt part, locked up from induſtry, in the hands of tackſmen. Might it not be enacted, that in every large town, or diſtrict of a certain extent on the ſea-ſhore, there ſhould be certain ſpots, or ſpaces, the moſt convenient for fiſhing, marked out, where, if any fiſher ſhould chuſe to ſettle, he ſhould have a right do ſo, on paying a certain ſmall quit-rent to the

---

* See particularly an " Eſſay on the Right of Property in Land, with reſpect to its Foundation in the Law of Nature; its preſent Eſtabliſhment by the Municipal Laws of Europe; and the Regulations by which it might be rendered more beneficial to the lower Ranks of mankind." I hope this little book will make its way to the attention of men who have it in their power to take ſome meaſures for carrying what is moſt practicable in that treatiſe, into execution.

the proprietor? Where cities, villages, or hamlets of refuge might be built, and where, in procefs of time, the voice of induftry, joy, and gladnefs might be heard, and at laft drown the groans and cries of misfortune, fmarting under the rod of oppreffion?

Without the interference of the law, wife proprietors of land, it would feem, fhould be naturally led to enfranchife fuch places, here and there on the coafts of the iflands, from a reafonable profpect of private advantage.

A noble example of this kind has been given by Mr. Mackenzie of Torridon, who, on a loch of that name, on the weftern coaft of Rofs-fhire, has taken the moft prudent, and I am glad to underftand, fuccefsful meafures for uniting a fifhery with a woollen manufactory.

Loch Torridon is fituated in 57 degrees and half North latitude. It is about twelve miles in length, and at a medium, two in breadth: though it be here and there indented by promontories of land, advancing at unequal diftances, into the water, and fometimes, joined to the main land only by a narrow ifthmus. Thefe irregularities afford advantages to the fifhermen, and concur, with rivers, woods, and mountains, to render the natural fcenery around Loch Torridon highly romantic and interefting. The margin of the loch is fringed by a ftrip of arable land of unequal width. The lower parts of the furrounding hills and mountains afford good pafture, where they are not covered with wood: and the fummits of the mountains, with the glens and moraffes intervening between them, are plentifully ftocked with various kinds of game. The rivers that fall into the lake are ftocked with falmon and various kinds of trout. In the loch there is the greateft abundance of merchantable fifh; and alfo great quantities of the fineft oyfters. This inlet of the fea is not only well fheltered and fpacious, but it has good holding ground, and is eafy of accefs. Several hundreds of the largeft veffels ride with fafety, in this natural harbour, in all weathers.

The natural advantages of this place invited the proprietor, Mr. Mackenzie, to add to thefe fuch improvements as might render it one of the moft commodious fifhing ftations that can be defired; and he has made fuch judicious and liberal arrangements, that men of property, or men of no property, provided they be induftrious, and of good morals, may carry on the fifhing bufinefs, with the greateft profpect of advantage. The enlarged views of Mr. Mackenzie begin to meet with their natural and juft reward in an increafed induftry on his eftate, and a refort to Torridon of many poor, but hard-working people. I wifh, with all my heart, that this effort of Mr. Mackenzie, for the eftablifhment of induftry and comfort in his neighbourhood, may fucceed. For one fuccefsful example will avail more towards the introduction of ufeful arts, than the moft juft reafoning, either in word or writing.

There is a ftation ftill more advantageous for fifhing than Torridon, that has hitherto been neglected, both by the proprietor and the Britifh Society: although Nature feems to prefs it on their attention, and imagination

tion itself cannot conceive a more inviting situation for maritime induſtry or exertion. The place to which I allude, as any one acquainted with the geography of the Hebrides will readily ſuppoſe, is the Tarbat: a narrow neck of land, connecting Lewis with Harris, and dividing the caſtern from the weſtern ſeas by a narrow iſthmus of ſix hundred paces. This is to the Hebrides what the Straits of Panama are to America.

CHAP.

## CHAP. IX.

*State of Religion in the Western Hebrides---Presbyteries---Synods---Missionaries---Elders---School Masters---Catechists.*

IN former times, as is well known, the Western Isles of Scotland, as well as Ireland, to which they were nearly adjacent, were distinguished as the retreats of pious and learned men, and, at one period, the chief seats of sanctity and of learning in Europe. For many years too, after the Reformation, and even so late as the middle of the present century, there was much sincerity and zeal in religious matters among the people in the Hebrides, as well as a strict discipline in the church. The clergy were exemplary in their lives, regular and conscientious in the discharge of their duty. They visited the sick, and spent much time in examining and praying with and for their people: ministerial duties which, at this day, are not fo much as named in the Weftern Hebrides; except indeed among the Catholic clergy, who are very affiduous in the difcharge of their religious functions, and therefore much beloved by the people; among whom their influence and authority is every day increafing. A laxity of morals prevails too much in the Eftablifhed Church, in general, (though there are a few exceptions) as well as of difcipline, minifters as well as elders,* being more intent on the acquirement or enjoyment of the good things of this life, than on any fpiritual objects. With regard to the great mafs of the people, fo much of their time is taken up in temporal avocations, in ploughing or digging their arable fpots of land, rearing cattle, making kelp, cutting peats, driving cattle for their mafters, and other fervices, that it is not in their power to affemble regularly together, in a fit frame for public worfhip: not to mention that it is chiefly on the Sundays, after the labour of the preceding

* A kind of lay brethren in the Church of Scotland, mingling, in fome meafure, the character and functions of the ancient catechifts and deacons, with thofe of Englifh overfeers of the poor and churchwardens.

ing week is over, that their mafters chufe to fend them on errands to diftant countries and iflands. Poor hard-working people, who, for want of time on the Saturday nights, are obliged to carry home their implements of hufbandry from their mafters houfes to their own cottages, every Sabbath morning, can hardly be fuppofed to travel fifteen miles more backward and forward, to hear a fermon; after being fatigued with their morning's journey of feven or eight miles, and that performed under a burthen. Indeed worldly cares and occupations, though not bodily labour, break in too often on the religious exercifes of the clergy themfelves as well as of the people.

*Prefbyteries* are held twice and fometimes thrice a year, for the purpofe of drawing up certificates for miffionaries, fchoolmafters, and minifters widows, and other bufinefs. At thefe meetings two muft make a quorum, as three or four clergymen are not to be found together at the fame prefbytery, unlefs compelled to meet by fome very urgent affair, or drawn together voluntarily by fome common intereft. The members of the

the prefbyteries in the ifles never debate and divide on any queftion before them, as in the more numerous or popular prefbyteries on the main land. There is no oppofition made by one minifter to the motion of his brother clergyman, whatever it be; and the other is as complaifant to him in his turn. This mutual complaifance, however, of the reverend gentlemen to one another, may be, and too frequently is, made an engine of oppreffion towards any perfon within the precincts of their fpiritual jurifdiction, who is fo unfortunate as to incur their difpleafure. Of fuch oppreffion I cannot but give one flagrant and even flagitious example. A private letter, written by a gentleman to a friend on the main land was intercepted. The very reverend gentleman who intercepted it made unjuft and malicious commentaries on fome lively expreffions which it contained, in a prefbytery; fubjected the innocent writer of the letter to a prefbyterial rebuke; and left the injured gentleman fhould have an opportunity of juftifying himfelf by a fair and confiftent explanation of his meaning, committed the letter to the flames.

*Presbyteries* are for the moſt part held at public houſes, and continued ſometimes without adjournment or prorogation for three ſucceſſive days and nights. The holy fathers ſtand in no need of Paul's advice to Timothy reſpecting his weak ſtomach. Their zeal in complying with that advice rather ſtands in need of moderation. In plain Engliſh, they are often carried, through the natural exigencies of a moiſt and cold climate, and their mutual joy at ſeeing one another, from ſuch diſtances of ſpace, and after ſuch intervals of time, to great exceſſes. One may form a judgment of their ſtile of living at the preſbyteries in the Weſtern Hebrides from the bill of fare, for one day, in a place where luxuries, as well as proviſions, are ſo cheap as in Harris. This was no leſs than one pound ſterling per head; or three pounds for the three days that the preſbytery laſted. —As the meetings of the preſbyteries are, for the moſt part, ſcenes of riot, they are attended only by young people of both ſexes, who delight in frolic.

Having ſaid ſo much of Hebridean preſbyteries in general, it is juſtice to obſerve, that
the

the clergy of Lewis attend the meetings of presbyteries regularly: and that these are not attended with such abominable excesses as mark the clerical assemblies in some other quarters. The town of Stornaway is full of strangers passing and repassing, who would be sure to entertain themselves and their acquaintance with a rehearsal of clerical riots, if they had any great handle for doing so. This, no doubt, is a check on the presbytery of Lewis: but, it must be confessed, that a greater decency of character begins to prevail here among the clergy than in the other isles composing the long chain of islands. And it is to be hoped, that the young men lately settled here by Mr. Mackenzie will adhere to the customs, manners, and regulations observed on the main land.

The same general observations here made on the western presbyteries may be justly extended to the synods, if I may judge from what I witnessed at that which met some years ago at Sky, the same defiance of decorum and propriety of conduct; the same contempt of the rules of the church; and the same disposition to carry every thing by combination. As one instance of tyranny, in the reverend synod,

synod, and disregard to the forms of justice, I shall mention one. The minister of Harris wished, as it was supposed, to exclude even as a spectator from the synod, the missionary minister of Harris, his colleague in sacred functions though not settled in the established church, and therefore without a vote in church judicaories. Although it be a rule in the Scottish ecclesiastical, as in all other well constituted Courts of Justice, to hold their sittings, with open doors, and in the face of the world, the established minister, it is said, from his spite against the missionary, had the shameless effrontery to make a motion, that the door of the synod should be shut against all strangers, or all who had not a seat and vote there; which motion was actually carried *nemine contradicente*. The strangers were accordingly dismissed, and the doors of the chamber, where the holy brethren met, locked hard and fast. The infrequency of presbyterial meetings, and the circumstance of their seldom consisting of more than two or three members, is a source of much trouble, vexation, and loss to the missionary ministers supported in the Western Isles by the Royal Bounty. It is a law or rule among the managers of that

P            charity

charity not to give the miffionary his annual ftipend, unlefs he produce a certificate of his good conduct and diligence. Now it is neceffary that the miffionary fhould either lie out of his ftipend for months after it becomes due, or perform a long journey in queft of thofe members who do not attend the prefbyteries, in order to get their fignatures to his certificate. It is impoffible for any man to pafs through Harris, from ifland to ifland, for a fignature, all the way to Barray, without lofing three weeks time, befides expences. This journey repeated annually, keeps the miffionary fix weeks from his duty. The fame hardfhips are incurred by fchoolmafters on the Royal Bounty.— There fhould, undoubtedly, be a ftated time, annually, when minifters, in order to complete the number of four, for the conveniency and benefit of the poor miffionaries and fchoolmafters, fhould make it a point of confcience and duty to attend the prefbyteries.

The miffionaries are neglected, or treated with hardfhip and unkindnefs at all hands, except among the poor oppreffed people among

among whom they are fent, who have but little time and opportunity allowed them, as has already been obferved, to liften to their inftructions, and whofe humble and hard fortune does not permit them to contribute in any material degree to their comfort and accommodation. They are neglected, and even treated with rigour by the managers of the bounty; and inftead of meeting with the countenance and favour of thofe whom they are fent to affift in the labour of the Lord, they are regarded, if they do their duty, with jealoufy and diflike. It is an eafy matter, and no uncommon thing among hypocrites, to fhew their regard to duty and religion, by a ftrict adherence to forms, when that adherence, however injurious to others, does not affect their own happinefs. Thus we have known political reformers who, without retrenching the enormous emoluments of their own, or the offices of their friends, made a merit of collecting and bringing into the public treafury the paltry clippings taken from poor officers of inferior ftations in the public fervice, whofe annual income did not exceed fifty pounds! I knew a miffionary clergyman, who, confcious of his

zeal

zeal in doing duty, and whofe character was univerfally refpected, ventured to fend his certificate to the managers at Edinburgh, figned only by the two minifters, who made up the prefbytery. A reverend baronet fent it back for more fignatures, which put the miffionary to a great deal of inconveniency, as well as lofs of time and unneceffary expence from dangerous ferries.

It is wonderful that fuch confcientious managers leave their miffionaries unprovided with any fixed habitations, or places of refidence, in the different iflands they are deftined to vifit: without which habitations it is impoffible that they can promote the end of their miffion. In the horrid ifland of Harris, no place of refidence has ever been thought of for the miffionary minifter, for forty years back, in a diftrict of twenty-feven miles in circuit, befides three iflands. The Englifh clergy are remarkably attentive to their mifficnaries, and grant no relief or affiftance to any country or diftrict, unlefs the inhabitants, on their part, encourage their miffionaries, not only with lodging, but alfo with a certain proportion of their maintenance.

Fcom

From the want of fixed habitations, the Hebridean missionaries, if they do their duty, as they sometimes have done, particularly the two last in the Harris district, are obliged to travel, sometimes twenty-four, and sometimes thirty-six miles a day, and that over the most rugged mountains.

I grant, that the journies of the clergyman might sometimes be shortened by navigation. But this could not be done with any degree of regularity, on account of the uncertainty of the weather, and sudden and dangerous squalls, in the fierce Atlantic Ocean, divided, broken, and confined, among islands parted into deep glens and lofty mountains. The good laird of Clanronald, sensible of the miserable situation of the missionaries, has built an excellent house for them in Benbicula, at his own expence.

The natural consequence of the neglect, on the part of the managers of the Royal Bounty, to send intelligent and upright visitors into the isles, who will not be cajoled by the blandishments of either hospitality or of flattery, to inspect the real state of religious

ligious affairs, and the circumstances of the
missionary as well as of the country and people. The natural consequence of this neglect, and particularly of sending the missionaries from place to place, like itinerant beggars, without any fixed residence, is, that the
subject of their mission is very imperfectly
fulfilled, when it is at all, which does not
often happen, attended to.

Yet, the most careless and indolent of the
missionaries can never be in want of the
most ample and formal certificates of their
good morals, industry, zeal, and success too,
in their clerical functions: nay, agreeably
to an observation I have already made, the
more careless and indolent the missionary, the
more likely he is to conciliate the favour---
at least to avoid the displeasure of the established clergy. The missionary of Harris,
according to the custom on the main land of
Scotland, began to visit, and pray with, and
examine the people committed to his charge,
from village to village: a practice hitherto
unknown in those parts. But that part of
of his duty he thought it prudent to give
up: as it gave offence to his colleague, who
considered

considered it as a libel on his own conduct.
Neither was the zeal of the missionary liked
by the tacksmen, who were unwilling that
the people, for any religious purposes, should
have the smallest respite from their labour.
The missionary being made an object of ridicule, and likely to undergo farther perse-
cution if he persisted in his plans for in-
structing and consoling the poor oppressed
people, by the hopes of religion, chose to
accommodate his conduct, in some measure,
to the taste of those among whom it was his
lot for some time to live.

I shall now say a few words on the subject
of the ELDERS in those remote regions, having
first added to what I have observed concerning
that class of men, above, that each parish, according to the constitution, sends what they
call a ruling elder to sit, and vote along with
the ministers in the presbyteries. *Elders*, in
the Hebrides, are, for the most part, mere nominal office-bearers: as they take no concern
about the spiritual state of the people; and, in
Kirk Courts vote, or are silent, just as their
minister, whose creatures they are, and who
increases, or, in fact, (for he cannot formally)

dimi-

diminifhes their number, as it fuits his intrigues, chufes to prefcribe. Indeed it would be a great curiofity to fee men in waiting, praying with, and comforting the fick, and watching over the morals of the people, as in feveral parts of the Lowlands of Scotland, who are themfelves moft irregular in their lives, and addicted, as they often, and even for the greater part, efpecially in Harris, to various kinds of debauchery. As for drunkennefs, though finful and fhameful in itfelf, it may, in fome meafure, be confidered as a vice incident to an almoft Hyperborean climate. But among Weft - Hebridean elders, there is nothing more common than concubinage, fornication, and even, adultery.

But from thefe general remarks on the character and condition of the elders in the Weft - Hebridean Iflands, I muft except thofe of North Uift, among whom are feveral refpectable gentlemen, ornaments to the church. It is obferved by a prophet, " As is the people, fo are the priefts." The converfe of this, equally true, may, perhaps, be applied to minifters and elders. " As is the

the minifter, fo is his Kirk-Seffion :" *—for this is of his own modifying and chufing.

I fhall here confirm what I have faid in general of the *elders* in the Long Ifland, by a well-known ftory, which may alfo, perhaps, be thought to illuftrate, in fome meafure, the ftate of fociety in the Weftern Hebrides among the common order of the people, in refpect of delicacy or indelicacy of fentiment. But, as I muft, in the courfe of that ftory, introduce the name of the minifter of Uig in a fort of comical manner, I muft premife, that this reverend gentleman is on the whole defervedly refpected: he is regular in preaching on Sundays, and on other days he is zealous in the fupport and promotion of good order in fociety. He is a terror to evil doers, particularly to dogs, whom, in general, he confiders as common thieves: many of thofe animals, in the Hebrides, being trained to the art of fheep-ftealing.

This

* The Kirk-Seffion is the loweft court in the church of of Scotland. It confifts of the minifter and the elders, who meet, and fettle little matters relating to the kirk and the poor, every week.

This reverend clergyman incurred no fmall degree of blame as well as ridicule for inconfiderately marrying an old adulterous elder from Harris, of the name of Macaulay, to a bafe woman whom he knew to be pregnant by another man. That other man wanted to marry the woman, and was very inftant in his folicitations for that end. But, as her affections were fcattered among the many fuitors who applied to her, and feldom altogether, in vain for favours, of whom the old elder was one, fhe did not well know how to decide upon the matter herfelf, but referred it to her father and mother. The prudent parents begged the fuitor, who believed himfelf to be the father of the child, to defift from all farther courtfhip of their daughter, as the old elder was a more eligible match, being richer; affuring him that, with regard to the infant with which fhe was pregnant, he fhould not be put to any farther trouble. He perfevered. Fond to diftraction of the woman, he thought to get rid of the old elder as a rival, by bluntly telling him to his face, that the woman he courted was with-child by himfelf. The elder was not eafily difgufted; but faid to the young

man,

man, that he would forgive him all the paſt, on condition that he would not keep company with her in future. But this the other would not promiſe! alledging many reaſons for not forgetting a perſon with whom he had been ſo long on terms of the greateſt intimacy.

He then went to the miniſter, to whom he related the whole hiſtory of his connection with the woman, from firſt to laſt. But, old Macaulay, in defiance of all the remonſtrances of the young man, had intereſt enough with the clergyman, who frequently reſided at his houſe, to perform the ceremony of marriage between him and this infamous woman, and to declare them married perſons.

The elder led his bride, far advanced, and bearing the moſt viſible and prominent marks of pregnancy, home to his houſe. The ſpectators laughed and jeered as they paſſed along: but old Macaulay comforted himſelf amidſt all their gibes, by ſaying, which he did again and again, " This veſſel is mine, whoever may claim the cargo."

This *elder* Macaulay had been married before; and in his firft wife's life-time kept a concubine in the houfe with him; by whom he had a daughter. To this daughter, defpifing his firft wife, he committed the charge of his family. A fon of his, begotten in adultery, keeps his cattle.

He has given other proofs of licentioufnefs of the fame kind: but no matter! He is rich, hofpitable, and extremely ufeful to the clergymen paffing, and repaffing his way, in lodging and entertaining them, helping them on their journeys with his boat, &c. He attends the kirk regularly, and keeps on good terms with his minifter.

The elders of the iflands never appear like thofe of the main land, at prefbyteries or fynods, unlefs they are preffed to come forward, by their minifter, on any important occafion, when fome meafure is to be fanctioned by as many votes as can be well obtained: nor do they ever prefume to give their opinion on any queftion, unlefs it be afked, and reduceable to a fingle aye, or no; or fo much as to fpeak the fofteft whifper,
until

until the bowl comes forward. Then, indeed, they begin to open their throats: and by and by their voice is raifed fo loud as to be fufficiently heard, and fometimes to drown that of the minifters.

There are in the Long Ifland two public fchools, maintained by the Royal Bounty, befides feveral fchools founded and endowed by private charities; both, from the vaft diftance between them, and what may be called the feat of their government, Edinburgh, (the refidence of the managers, a committee chofen annually by the General Affembly of the Church of Scotland, which meets every year towards the end of May) very much abufed.

A fum of twenty-five pounds per annum was granted by the managers of the Royal Bounty, for teaching a grammar fchool at Stornaway in Lewis. But, during the abfence of the late laird of Lewis, Colonel Humberftone Mackenzie, in the Eaft-Indies, the minifter of Stornaway had influence enough with the managers of the Bounty to convert the twenty-five pounds into a falary for a miffionary,

onary, who might act as an affiftant, and eafe the minifter of part of his parochial duty.

The prefent H. Mackenzie, moved by the juft complaints of the merchants of Stornaway, applied to the managers, and had influence enough to get the money reftored to its original purpofe.

There is at prefent a very good fchool in Stornaway. The parochial fund, or dues, added to the Royal Bounty, make up together a very good livelihood for the fchoolmafter. Mr. Mackenzie and the inhabitants of Stornaway very juftly confidered, that a fchoolmafter might be more ufefully employed in training up the young, than a miffionary in preaching to the old.

The only fchool in all the Ifland of Harris is the parifh fchool at Roudle, brought thither from Scarafta, where it ftood before, by the late proprietor, when he wanted to collect inhabitants for raifing a village. Throughout the whole of the back fettlements of Harris, where the poor people have been driven by degrees from the *machar,*

*char*, or plain lands, a diſtrict of thirty-ſix miles in length, and from four to five in breadth, all the way from Roudle to Huſkiniſh, planted thick with inhabitants, the people never once had an offer or opportunity of education for their children, although funds had been provided, and ſet apart, by the charity of individuals, for that purpoſe. But the charitable funds were always detained, by the miniſter, or better ſort of people in the iſle, and never made their way acroſs the mountains. The nominal charity ſchool-maſters, however, had always found means to obtain certificates for the purpoſe of drawing their ſalaries, till a half-pay Lieutenant, Lewis Macgregor, alias Drummond, a religious and conſcientious man, was ſent, about fifteen years ago, as a viſitant of the ſchools, by the managers.

Captain Macgregor finding the poor in Harris groſsly ignorant, and wholly neglected, ordered the money to be withdrawn, and recomended it to be employed otherwiſe.

The money deſigned to ſupport charity-ſchools in that country had either been given to natives, who neither troubled themſelves about

about the poor, nor were qualified to inftruct the children of thofe in better circumftances: or to ftrangers, who were ftationed either befide the minifter, if he had a family, or, if he had not, in the fmall ifles for the benefit of gentlemen's children; but never either at Tarbat, the moft central part, and the moft fitted for intercourfe in all the Long Ifland, in the middle of Harris, and in the heart of the real poor, for whom the charity was intended.

A gentleman of the name of Macleod funk, or, according to the Scottifh phrafeology mortified a yearly fum of twelve pounds to be given to fome native of Harris, and of his own name, (Macleod) for teaching the illiterate to repeat the creed and Lord's prayer, and to anfwer theological queftions by rote, in Gâlic, and explain their meaning. But the gentleman, who had intereft to fecure this money from the managers at Edinburgh, to whom the charge of it is very injudicioufly intrufted, has two or more valuable farms to manage; and therefore cannot fpend above a week or a fortnight in the year

in

in travelling over the parish, to inquire at the people concerning the attendance of his two substitutes. The one of these is an old blind beggar, of fourscore years and upwards, who is led by the hand by any boy or girl, or other person who will have the goodness to do so, from village to village, and from door to door. The other is a decrepid changeling, but endowed with a tenacious memory. The minister of Harris married the poor creature to a dirty old trull, who might, if possible, keep him tolerably clean in his person. The disgusting figure of this mendicant teacher of religion may be conceived from the following anecdote:

When the late Sir John Elliot, who resided some time on the island of Harris for the recovery of his health, happened to see this changeling, who intruded into the room in which Sir John was sitting, he was so shocked at his appearance, as to be ready to fall into fits, and instantly ordered him from his presence. What respect such instructors can reflect on religion, and what success they can have in teaching it, it is not difficult to imagine. Each of these worthy substi-

substitutes has the promise from their principal, Macleod, of ten shillings a year; which, however, it is said, is performed only in words. They are literally beggars; and depend for support solely on the alms of the poor people among whom they sojourn. This species of teachers is, in those parts, called *Questars*.

Lord Macdonald has obtained, from the managers of the Royal Bounty, twenty or twenty-five pounds for the establishment of a school in North Uist, which, like that in Stornaway, is united with the parish-school, making together a very comfortable subsistence. The minister of Harris, imitating the policy above mentioned of the minister of Stornaway, attempted to convert this fund into a salary for an assistant to himself in Harris. But his design, through the vigilance of Lord Macdonald and the gentlemen in North Uist, was frustrated.

There were, formerly, two charity-schools in *South Uist:* the one taught by a Mr. Wright, alias Mackintyre; the other by a Mr. Chrystie: both of them strangers, conscientious

scientious and diligent in their profeſſion. But, being ſtationed among Roman Catholics, fighting againſt the ſtream, and unſupported by the preſbytery, who uſed no means to enforce the conditions on which charity-ſchools were planted among the inhabitants of that iſland, they returned to the main land with the melancholy complaint of poverty and neglect. Mr. Chryſtie was forced to leave his wife behind him, until Providence ſhould prepare ſome aſylum.

Similar complaints are made, and with equal reaſon, by the poor charity-ſchoolmaſter of Barra, who is alſo ſtationed in the midſt of Papiſts; and whoſe miniſter neither gives himſelf any trouble about the ſituation of the ſchoolmaſter, nor indeed, could be of much ſervice to him, with his Popiſh pariſhioners, by whom he is very little reſpected, if he did. This poor ſchoolmaſter earneſtly wiſhes to go with his ragged, ſtarved, and moſt miſerable looking family, to the main land; but he wants the means for tranſportation.

There was formerly a little fchool in the Ifle of Bernera, until the fchoolmafter quitted his charge, and enlifted as a private in the army.

As to the order of *Queſtars*, in the Hebrides, on which I have already touched, that go about from houfe to houfe, teaching the children the Creed, the Commandments, &c. by rote, in the evenings, they are not only ufelefs, but many of them worthlefs drunkards.

There is a blind bully of this order in *Uiſt*, who, in order to efcape contempt, and fecure refpectful attention both to his perfon and his doctrines, carries about with him, wherever he goes, loaded piftols. As he is remarkably ſtrong, as well as full of courage, though blind, few people are fond of grappling with him.

In general, I have to obferve on charity-fchools, that the fund appropriated to thofe feminaries are fometimes of great benefit to minifters and tackfmen, who can afford to pay for the education of their children: but

very

very seldom to the poor people for whose benefit they were intended. Indeed there is plainly, a diposition among what is called the better sort of people in the islands, to keep the poor and labouring people in ignorance, that they may be the more tractable and submissive. And, on the whole of this view of the present state of the Western Hebrides, there is one reflection which constantly recurs, and remains uppermost in the mind: namely, that there is, in that unhappy region, a melancholy degree of religious neglect and political oppression. The first of these positions is emphatically proved by the increase of Popery, in those islands, particularly the most southerly of them: the second, by the emigration of the people, whenever they have an opportunity. With all our royal bounties, and private charities, we are not so succesful in our religious labours as the Papists: among whom there is sincerity and zeal, and a reciprocal affection between pastor and people.

The synod of Glenelg may save themselves the trouble of asking the missionaries annually what number of Protestants they have

have made? The anſwer to which queſtions, uniformly, is none. A very different anſwer muſt be made, if the queſtion were put, How many hearers they had loſt?

I here beg leave to ſuggeſt two things to the reverend managers of the Royal Bounty, and the General Aſſembly, under whoſe authority they act, both of which ſeem to be eaſily practicable. To aim at a general reform among the clergy, and the ſettlement of ſuch men only in church livings as would vie with the Popiſh miniſters in the Long Iſland, in purity of manners, and zeal for the propagation of religion, would be idle and chimerical. But very much depends in ſuch extenſive pariſhes, and among ſo uncultivated a people, upon the character and conduct of the *elders* in their reſpective quarters. The miniſters of the pariſhes ought therefore to be ſtrictly enjoined, under pain of ſuſpenſion, and, in caſe of contumacy, even of depoſition, not to admit, or ſuffer to remain in their Kirk Seſſions, any open and habitual adulterers, whore-mongers, profane ſwearers, breakers of the Sabbath, extortioners, or oppreſſors: nor yet, if it be poſſible poffible to form a fhew of Kirk feffions otherwife, notorious drunkards.

The other hint I would give to the reverend managers, is, to be more careful than they ufually have been, who they fend to the iflands as vifitants. The iflanders are an acute, fhrewd, and penetrating people: they have, particularly, a quick difcrimination of character; and if a man has a weak fide, as moft men have, they will readily difcover it, and practife on it with great fuccefs. If avarice be his ruling paffion, they will footh him with fuch prefents as they can make; if he is addicted to the pleafures of the table, they will ply him inceffantly with good cheer and generous liquors; and, as Dr. Thompfon fays, if he be notorioufly felf-conceited, and felf-important, they will flatter his vanity.

It has fometimes happened, as I have been told, that the managers, in their choice of a vifitant, have been more attentive to the wifhes and importunities of certain buftling, reftlefs, and intriguing fpirits, who wanted to have a poft, and a Summer excurfion, curſion, free of expence, than to the qualities of his mind.

I have heard of a viſitant who had no other motive for ſoliciting the appointment, than that he wiſhed to have a reſpite for ſome months, from being hen-pecked by his wife. That appointment the clergyman alluded to certainly received, although, what will appear incredible, he was ignorant of the Gâlic tongue.

Let us ſuppoſe ſuch a viſitant arrived in any of the iſlands---Harris, for example:---He is moſt hoſpitably entertained by the miniſter, and the tackſman of Luſkintire, careſſed, humoured, cajoled, and flattered, with all manner of adulation. He paſſes on to ſome other iſle with letters of introduction from theſe gentlemen to their friends, who treat him in the ſame manner; and ſo on, with letters from them to the lairds, miniſters, and tackſmen of ſome other iſland. He is kept in a conſtant round of entertainment, I had almoſt ſaid, of diſſipation. He lives with thoſe in eaſy and affluent circumſtances: he hears their tale, and theirs only:

fees

fees only the fair face of things: and, inftead of exploring, and feeling for the religious neglect, and civil oppreffion of the great body of the people, returns home, highly delighted with his jaunt and reception; and is even apt to reprefent the poor, miferable Æbudæ as the fortunate iflands, in the Atlantic Ocean, fpoken of by the ancients, although their exact geographical fituation had never before been determined.

With regard to the means proper to be ufed for the gradual abolition of predial fervitude in the Hebrides, I have already faid, that Government fhould do every thing, that may be eafily done, for the facilitation of the Fifheries, not only at a few fcattered ftations, but throughout the whole range of the various and extenfive fhores of the iflands, wherever commodious creeks and bays, and other inlets of the fea, attract the fifhes, and prompt the endeavours of the natives to catch them.

I fhall conclude thefe remarks on the Long Ifland, by joining my feeble voice to that of thofe those patriotic and enlightened men who have written, not only against entails, but the excessive monopolization of land, by great farmers. The evil of such a monopolization was obvious to men of candid and liberal minds, in Scotland, more than three hundred years ago. David Stewart, of the family of Lorn, bishop of Murray, from 1458 to 1460, among several good regulations, enacted, " that the common kirk (church) lands be let to none but the labourers of the ground; and that no pensions be paid out of the same."

It would be impracticable, in the present situation and circumstances of society, to adopt and extend the good bishop's law over all the landed property of Great Britain. But, it would well become the wisdom of the Legislature to take such measures as might have a tendency to raise the industrious labourer, from the situation of being a servant to another man, to one in which he might have the satisfaction of cultivating the soil on his own account.

That

That this might be be done in various ways, by a wife and vigilant Legiſlature, without occaſioning any ſudden and violent change in the minds or ſituation of any of the orders of ſociety, has been clearly and fully demonſtrated by the philoſophers and patriots whom I have already quoted on this ſubject, and whoſe reaſoning has been, I underſtand, very generally, if not univerſally approved by their readers.

FINIS.

www.ingramcontent.com/pod-product-compliance
Lightning Source LLC
Chambersburg PA
CBHW032205230426

43672CB00011B/2522